C000129586

"Rise & Fall of Ancient Civilizations, and the False Matrix"

David Jack Gregg

Copyright © 2023 Tremendous Prints
All rights reserved.

CONTENTS

In "Rise & Fall of Ancient Civilizations, and the False Matrix," we embark on a captivating journey through the annals of history to explore the rise, triumphs, and eventual decline of remarkable ancient civilizations. Alongside this historical narrative, we delve into a thought-provoking exploration of the concept of a "False Matrix" – a metaphorical construct that challenges our perceptions of reality and invites introspection into the nature of truth and human existence.

In "Rise & Fall of Ancient Civilizations, and the False Matrix," we have embarked on an extraordinary voyage through the rise, triumphs, and eventual decline of remarkable ancient civilizations.

Chapter 1: The Birth of Civilization

Introduction: In Chapter 1, "The Birth of Civilization," we delve into the origins of human civilization and the remarkable advancements that led to the rise of early societies. We explore the transition from nomadic hunter-gatherer lifestyles to settled agricultural communities, a pivotal moment in human history that laid the foundation for the development of complex civilizations.

Section 1: Prehistoric Beginnings In this section, we travel back in time to the Paleolithic era, where our ancestors roamed the earth as nomadic hunter-gatherers. We explore the challenges they faced in their quest for survival and examine the gradual transition from a purely subsistence-based lifestyle to more settled communities.

Section 2: The Agricultural Revolution Here, we delve into the revolutionary discovery of agriculture and its transformative impact on human societies. We investigate the development of agriculture in different regions of the world, such as the Fertile Crescent in Mesopotamia, the Nile River Valley in Egypt, and the Indus Valley in South Asia. We analyze the cultivation of crops, the domestication of animals, and the emergence of sedentary lifestyles.

Section 3: Early Urbanization In this section, we witness the birth of early cities and the establishment of urban centers as hubs of economic, political, and cultural activities. We examine the growth of city-states, such as Uruk in Mesopotamia and Mohenjo-daro in the Indus Valley, and explore the factors that facilitated urbanization, including trade, specialization of labor, and the development of social hierarchies.

Section 4: Written Language and Record Keeping Here, we delve into the emergence of written language as a revolutionary tool for communication and record keeping. We explore the earliest writing systems, such as cuneiform in Mesopotamia and hieroglyphics in ancient Egypt, and analyze the impact of writing on the preservation and transmission of knowledge, the administration of early states, and the development of literature.

Section 5: Technological Advancements In this section, we examine the technological advancements that accompanied the birth of civilization. We delve into the inventions and innovations that revolutionized ancient societies, such as the wheel, irrigation systems, metallurgy, and architectural techniques. We explore how these advancements enabled the construction of monumental structures, improved agricultural productivity, and enhanced trade and transportation.

Section 6: Social and Cultural Developments Here, we explore the social and cultural developments that shaped early civilizations. We investigate the emergence of social hierarchies, the division of labor, and the establishment of governance systems. We also delve into the religious beliefs, artistic expressions, and cultural practices that defined the identities of these early societies.

Conclusion: In conclusion, Chapter 1 provides a comprehensive exploration of the birth of civilization, tracing the journey from nomadic hunter-gatherer societies to the establishment of settled agricultural communities. We witness the revolutionary advancements in agriculture, urbanization, written language, technology, and social structures that set the stage for the remarkable civilizations that would follow. Through this exploration, we gain a deeper appreciation for the ingenuity and resilience of our ancestors and the profound impact of their achievements on the course of human history.

Section 1: Prehistoric Beginnings

In this section, we travel back in time to the Paleolithic era, a period that spans from around 2.6 million years ago to approximately 10,000 BCE. It was during this time that our early human ancestors first appeared on the stage of prehistory. These early humans were nomadic hunter-gatherers, constantly on the move in search of food and resources.

The Paleolithic era was characterized by a harsh and unpredictable environment. Our ancestors faced numerous challenges, including harsh climates, predatory animals, and the scarcity of food sources. Survival depended on their ability to adapt and innovate, and over time, they developed remarkable skills and techniques that allowed them to thrive.

One of the key characteristics of the Paleolithic era was the use of simple stone tools. Early humans crafted tools from rocks, shaping them into sharp edges for cutting, scraping, and hunting. These tools not only aided in hunting and gathering food but also served as multipurpose instruments for various tasks.

In terms of sustenance, early humans were primarily hunters and gatherers. They relied on their hunting skills to capture animals for meat, while also gathering edible plants, fruits, nuts, and seeds. Cooperation within groups was essential for successful hunting and gathering, as it required coordination, division of labor, and the sharing of resources.

The social structure of these early human groups was likely based on kinship ties and shared responsibilities. They lived in small bands or tribes, with strong bonds formed among family members and close-knit communities. Communication was crucial for survival, and early humans developed simple forms of language and communication systems to convey messages and coordinate their actions.

As the Paleolithic era progressed, humans began to exhibit signs of cultural development. They expressed themselves through cave paintings, rock art, and other forms of artistic expression. These artistic creations not only served as a means of communication but also provided a glimpse into their beliefs, rituals, and daily lives.

It is important to note that the Paleolithic era was not a homogeneous period across the globe. Different regions experienced unique environmental conditions, which influenced the lifestyles and adaptations of early humans. For example, those living in colder regions had to contend with harsh winters and developed specialized tools and clothing to withstand the cold.

Overall, Section 1 provides a fascinating insight into the prehistoric beginnings of human civilization. It highlights the resourcefulness and adaptability of our early ancestors as they navigated the challenges of their environment. This section sets the stage for the subsequent developments that would lead to the birth of agriculture and the emergence of settled civilizations in the chapters to come.

Section 2: The Agricultural Revolution

In this section, we delve into the revolutionary discovery of agriculture and its transformative impact on human societies. The Agricultural Revolution marks a significant turning point in human history, as it led to the transition from a nomadic, hunter-gatherer lifestyle to a settled, agricultural way of life.

The Agricultural Revolution began around 10,000 BCE and occurred independently in various regions of the world. It was during this time that humans discovered the practice of cultivating crops and domesticating animals, which provided a more stable and sustainable food source. This shift from a reliance on hunting and gathering to agriculture had profound implications for human societies.

The Fertile Crescent, a region encompassing present-day Iraq, Syria, and parts of Turkey, is considered one of the earliest centers of agricultural innovation. The ancient inhabitants of this region began to cultivate cereal crops such as wheat and barley, and they domesticated animals like sheep, goats, and cattle.

This agricultural surplus allowed for a more settled way of life, as people established permanent villages and developed complex social structures.

Similarly, in the Nile River Valley in ancient Egypt, the annual flooding of the river provided fertile soil for agriculture. The ancient Egyptians developed advanced irrigation systems to harness the water and cultivate crops such as wheat, barley, and flax. The agricultural abundance of the Nile River Valley supported the growth of a highly organized civilization that thrived for thousands of years.

In the Indus Valley, located in present-day Pakistan and northwest India, early farmers cultivated crops such as wheat, barley, rice, and cotton. They developed sophisticated systems of irrigation and urban planning, creating well-organized cities with advanced drainage systems. The agricultural surplus allowed for the emergence of a complex society with distinctive cultural and artistic achievements.

The discovery of agriculture brought about several significant changes. First and foremost, it provided a stable food supply, reducing the uncertainty and vulnerability associated with hunting and gathering. This surplus allowed for population growth, as communities could support larger numbers of individuals. It also led to the development of specialized labor, as people could focus on tasks beyond food procurement, such as pottery-making, weaving, and metalworking.

Agriculture also played a crucial role in the development of settled communities and the establishment of permanent dwellings. Instead of being constantly on the move in search of food, people could now reside in one place and cultivate the land. This led to the construction of houses, storage facilities, and other infrastructure necessary for a settled lifestyle.

The impact of the Agricultural Revolution extended beyond food production and settlement patterns. It brought about social changes as well, with the emergence of social hierarchies and the development of more complex political systems. Surpluses of agricultural resources allowed for the accumulation of wealth and the rise of specialized roles such as priests, rulers, and artisans.

In conclusion, Section 2 highlights the transformative power of the Agricultural Revolution. The transition from a nomadic lifestyle to agriculture-based settlements revolutionized human societies, providing a stable food supply, promoting population growth, and fostering the development of complex social structures. The discoveries and innovations of early farmers laid the groundwork for the emergence of civilizations and set the stage for further advancements in human history.

Section 3: Early Urbanization

In this section, we explore the birth of early cities and the establishment of urban centers as hubs of economic, political, and cultural activities. The process of urbanization, driven by the advancements in agriculture and the growth of settled communities, marked a significant milestone in the development of ancient civilizations.

One notable example of early urbanization can be found in ancient Mesopotamia, specifically in the region known as the Fertile Crescent. Cities such as Uruk, Ur, and Babylon emerged as centers of political power, trade, and cultural exchange. These cities were characterized by their impressive architecture, including monumental structures such as ziggurats and palaces, and their bustling markets and social gathering places.

The Indus Valley civilization also witnessed the rise of urban centers, most notably in cities like Mohenjo-daro and Harappa. These cities showcased a sophisticated urban planning system, with well-laid-out streets, brick houses, public baths, and an advanced sewage and drainage system. The Indus Valley cities were centers of trade and commerce, as evidenced by their well-organized marketplaces and the presence of standardized weights and measures.

Egypt, along the Nile River, saw the emergence of cities such as Memphis and Thebes. These cities were not only political and administrative centers but also served as religious and cultural hubs. The ancient Egyptians built monumental structures such as temples and tombs, reflecting their religious beliefs and honoring their rulers. The Nile River played a crucial role in the development of these cities, serving as a transportation route and providing fertile land for agriculture.

The process of urbanization brought about numerous changes in the fabric of society. Cities became melting pots of diverse cultures, attracting people from different regions and fostering the exchange of ideas, goods, and technologies. Specialization of labor became more pronounced, as individuals began to focus on specific trades and crafts, contributing to the overall prosperity of the city.

Urban centers also facilitated the development of centralized governance systems. Political authority became more concentrated in the hands of rulers, who governed the city-states and enacted laws and regulations to maintain order and manage resources. Temples often played a central role in the political and economic life of cities, serving as places of worship, administrative centers, and repositories of knowledge.

Trade and commerce flourished in urban settings, as cities became hubs for the exchange of goods and services. Markets and bazaars bustled with activity, bringing together merchants, craftsmen, and customers from near and far. The growth of trade networks, both within and between civilizations, led to the exchange of goods, ideas, and cultural influences, contributing to the enrichment and diversity of urban life.

In conclusion, Section 3 highlights the phenomenon of early urbanization and its profound impact on the development of ancient civilizations. The emergence of cities as centers of economic, political, and cultural activities brought about transformative changes in society, including the specialization of labor, the growth of centralized governance systems, and the flourishing of trade and cultural exchange. These early urban centers laid the foundation for the complex cities and societies that would follow in the course of human history.

Section 4: Written Language and Record Keeping

In this section, we delve into the emergence of written language as a revolutionary tool for communication and record keeping. The development of writing systems played a pivotal role in the preservation and transmission of knowledge, the administration of early states, and the flourishing of literature and intellectual pursuits.

One of the earliest known writing systems is cuneiform, which originated in ancient Mesopotamia around 3200 BCE. Cuneiform was a wedge-shaped script that used clay tablets as a medium for writing. Initially, it served primarily as a system for recording economic transactions and administrative matters. Over time, cuneiform expanded to encompass a wide range of topics, including historical accounts, legal codes, religious texts, and literary compositions.

In ancient Egypt, hieroglyphics emerged as a complex writing system around 3200 BCE. Hieroglyphics consisted of pictorial symbols that represented words, sounds, or concepts. They were predominantly inscribed on stone monuments, temple walls, and papyrus scrolls. Hieroglyphics were used for recording historical events, religious rituals, and administrative records, as well as for creating literary works such as poetry and myths.

The Indus Valley civilization also had a script that remains undeciphered to this day. The script, found on seals and pottery, indicates the presence of a writing system in the region. However, the complexities of the script and the limited number of surviving texts have made it challenging to decipher and understand the full extent of the Indus Valley script.

The development of written language revolutionized human societies in numerous ways. It allowed for the preservation of knowledge and the transmission of information across generations. Written records served as repositories of historical accounts, scientific discoveries, and cultural practices, ensuring that valuable insights were not lost to time. Additionally, written language facilitated the spread of ideas, as written texts could be copied and circulated, reaching wider audiences and sparking intellectual exchanges.

Written language played a crucial role in the administration of early states and empires. It enabled the creation of legal codes, administrative records, and official correspondence. Rulers and administrators relied on written documents to maintain control over their territories, collect taxes, and enforce laws. Written records also facilitated trade and commerce by documenting transactions, contracts, and inventories.

Moreover, the emergence of written language paved the way for the development of literature and artistic expression. Ancient civilizations produced epic poems, religious texts, philosophical treatises, and scientific observations. These literary works provided insight into the beliefs, values, and aspirations of ancient societies, while also showcasing the creativity and intellectual pursuits of their authors.

The impact of written language extended beyond the practical and intellectual realms. It played a crucial role in shaping cultural identities and fostering a sense of collective memory. Through the written word, myths, legends, and historical accounts were passed down, solidifying the shared narratives and cultural heritage of ancient civilizations.

In conclusion, Section 4 highlights the significance of written language in the ancient world. The development of writing systems, such as cuneiform and hieroglyphics, revolutionized communication, record keeping, administration, and literature. Written language became a powerful tool for preserving knowledge, shaping cultural identities, and advancing intellectual pursuits. The legacy of these early writing systems continues to influence and inspire modern civilizations.

Section 5: Technological Innovations and Engineering Marvels

In this section, we explore the technological innovations and engineering marvels that emerged in ancient civilizations. From impressive architectural achievements to groundbreaking inventions, ancient societies showcased remarkable ingenuity and engineering prowess.

One of the most iconic architectural marvels of the ancient world is the Great Pyramid of Giza in Egypt. Built during the Old Kingdom period around 2560 BCE, the pyramid stands as a testament to the Egyptians' advanced knowledge of engineering and construction. Its massive stone blocks, precisely aligned corners, and intricate internal passages continue to astound scholars and visitors alike.

Another engineering feat is the city of Rome, capital of the Roman Empire. The Romans revolutionized engineering by constructing monumental structures such as aqueducts, roads, and bridges. The aqueducts, a marvel of ancient engineering, transported water from distant sources to supply cities, enabling urban growth and improved sanitation. The Roman road network, known as the "viae," facilitated trade, communication, and military conquests, linking various parts of the empire.

In ancient China, significant advancements in engineering were made during the Han Dynasty (206 BCE to 220 CE). The construction of the Great Wall of China stands as a testament to the engineering skills of the time. This massive fortification system, stretching over thousands of miles, incorporated stone and brick walls, watchtowers, and other defensive structures. It served as protection against invasions and symbolized the might of the Chinese empire.

The ancient Greeks contributed to engineering with their architectural achievements and scientific innovations. The Parthenon, a temple dedicated to the goddess Athena, exemplifies Greek architectural excellence. Its harmonious proportions, intricate sculptural details, and innovative use of columns made it a masterpiece of classical architecture. Greek mathematicians and scientists, such as Archimedes, made groundbreaking discoveries and inventions, including the lever, pulley systems, and the concept of buoyancy.

In India, the ancient civilization of the Indus Valley showcased remarkable engineering skills. The city of Mohenjo-daro featured an advanced urban planning system, with well-constructed brick buildings, sophisticated drainage systems, and public baths. The Harrapan civilization also developed an early form of standardized weights and measures, indicating their understanding of precision and accuracy in trade and commerce.

Technological innovations extended beyond architecture and infrastructure. Ancient civilizations made significant advancements in various fields, such as medicine, mathematics, and metallurgy. The ancient Egyptians practiced rudimentary surgical procedures and developed remedies for various ailments. Babylonian mathematicians laid the foundation for advanced mathematical concepts, including the concept of zero and the development of the base-60 numeral system. Metallurgy played a crucial role in ancient societies, with advancements in metalworking leading to the production of tools, weapons, and decorative objects.

The technological innovations and engineering marvels of ancient civilizations have left a lasting impact on human history. They not only reflect the ingenuity and problem-solving abilities of these societies but also demonstrate their dedication to creating lasting structures and improving their quality of life. These advancements set the stage for further technological progress and paved the way for the modern world we live in today.

In conclusion, Section 5 highlights the technological achievements and engineering wonders of ancient civilizations. From the towering pyramids of Egypt to the intricate aqueducts of Rome, these civilizations showcased their engineering prowess and innovative spirit. The legacy of their technological innovations continues to inspire and influence the advancements of the present age.

Section 6: Social and Cultural Developments:

In the ever-evolving tapestry of ancient civilizations, social and cultural developments played a pivotal role in shaping the fabric of society. This section delves into the diverse aspects of social structure, belief systems, artistic expressions, and technological advancements that emerged during this transformative era. From the hierarchies of power to the emergence of new religious and philosophical ideologies, we explore the fascinating social and cultural dynamics that defined ancient civilizations.

Social Hierarchies: Ancient civilizations were characterized by distinct social hierarchies that delineated the roles and responsibilities of individuals within society. From the ruling elite and nobility to the laborers and slaves, each stratum had its place and function. We examine the structures and dynamics of these social hierarchies, shedding light on the power dynamics and social inequalities prevalent in ancient societies.

Religious and Philosophical Beliefs: Religion played a central role in the lives of ancient civilizations, shaping their beliefs, values, and rituals. We explore the diverse religious and philosophical systems that flourished during this time, from the polytheistic pantheons of the Egyptians and Greeks to the monotheistic faiths of Judaism and Zoroastrianism. Dive into the myths, rituals, and spiritual practices that provided meaning and guidance to ancient communities.

Art and Architecture: The artistic expressions of ancient civilizations offer profound insights into their cultural values, aesthetic sensibilities, and technical achievements. We delve into the monumental architecture, intricate sculptures, vibrant paintings, and exquisite craftsmanship that adorned temples, palaces, and public spaces. Discover the stories and symbolism embedded in these artistic creations, revealing the cultural aspirations and societal ideals of ancient peoples.

Technological Advancements: Ancient civilizations were not only repositories of cultural and artistic achievements but also pioneers in technological innovations. We explore the remarkable advancements made in areas such as agriculture, engineering, metallurgy, and medicine. From the construction of awe-inspiring structures to the development of irrigation systems, these technological feats revolutionized the way ancient societies functioned.

Gender Roles and Family Life: The study of social and cultural developments would be incomplete without examining the roles and expectations placed on individuals based on their gender. We delve into the complex dynamics of gender relations, marriage customs, and family structures prevalent in ancient civilizations. Uncover the varied experiences of men and women, and how societal norms shaped their opportunities and limitations.

Education and Intellectual Pursuits: Intellectual life and education held a significant place in ancient civilizations. We explore the centers of learning, such as the renowned Library of Alexandria, and the intellectual pursuits of scholars, philosophers, and mathematicians. Discover the philosophical systems, scientific discoveries, and literary masterpieces that emerged during this era of intellectual enlightenment.

Leisure and Entertainment: In addition to the serious aspects of social and cultural life, we also delve into the leisure activities and forms of entertainment that provided respite and enjoyment for ancient peoples. From theater performances and sporting events to music, dance, and games, we explore the diverse ways in which ancient civilizations engaged in leisure and recreation.

By delving into the intricate tapestry of social and cultural developments, we gain a deeper understanding of the complexities and nuances of ancient civilizations. These developments not only influenced the lives of individuals within those societies but continue to shape our own social and cultural landscapes today.

Chapter 2: The Rise of an Empire

In the vast landscape of ancient Mesopotamia, a powerful empire emerged, destined to shape the course of history. This chapter unveils the rise of the Babylonian Empire, led by the ambitious and visionary ruler, Hammurabi.

As the successor of the Akkadian and Sumerian civilizations, Babylon rose to prominence under the rule of Hammurabi, a charismatic and astute leader. Born into a noble family, Hammurabi ascended to the throne of Babylon in 1792 BCE. He was determined to establish a centralized and powerful empire that would stand the test of time.

Hammurabi understood the significance of a well-defined legal system for maintaining order and ensuring the loyalty of his subjects. He embarked on an ambitious project, known as the Code of Hammurabi, a comprehensive set of laws that covered various aspects of society, from commerce and property rights to marriage and inheritance. This code became the cornerstone of Babylonian society and established Hammurabi as a ruler dedicated to justice and fairness.

Under Hammurabi's rule, Babylon experienced a period of prosperity and cultural flourishing. The city became a hub of trade and commerce, attracting merchants and artisans from across the region. The economy thrived, fueled by agricultural surplus, skilled craftsmanship, and a network of trade routes that connected Babylon to distant lands.

Architecturally, Babylon underwent a transformation, with Hammurabi commissioning the construction of grand temples, palaces, and defensive walls. The city's most famous structure, the magnificent Ishtar Gate, adorned with vibrant blue glazed bricks and adorned with intricate animal reliefs, became a symbol of Babylonian grandeur.

Beyond his administrative and architectural achievements, Hammurabi also focused on expanding the borders of his empire. Through a series of military campaigns and strategic alliances, he conquered and assimilated neighboring city-states, gradually establishing Babylon as the dominant power in the region. Hammurabi's military successes were attributed to his ability to inspire loyalty among his troops and his strategic acumen in warfare.

However, the story of Hammurabi's empire was not without challenges. As the Babylonian Empire grew in size, managing the diverse cultures and regions under its rule proved to be a formidable task. Hammurabi employed a policy of cultural assimilation, allowing conquered peoples to retain their customs and traditions, as long as they pledged loyalty to Babylon. This approach helped to maintain stability but also presented ongoing challenges in terms of governance and cultural integration.

Chapter 2 unveils the rise of the Babylonian Empire under Hammurabi's visionary leadership. It explores the political, economic, and cultural achievements of Babylon during this golden age, highlighting Hammurabi's commitment to justice, the flourishing of trade and craftsmanship, and the expansion of the empire through military conquests. The chapter also delves into the complexities of managing a diverse empire and the ongoing efforts to maintain stability and cultural cohesion.

Chapter 3: Shadows of Power

As the Babylonian Empire entered a new era under Hammurabi's successors, the shadows of power and internal conflicts began to cast a long and uncertain shadow over the empire. This chapter unravels the challenges faced by Babylon and the subsequent decline of the once-mighty empire.

After the death of Hammurabi, his successors struggled to maintain the same level of stability and leadership. The empire faced internal power struggles and external threats from rival city-states and nomadic tribes. As a result, the centralized governance and unity that characterized Hammurabi's reign began to erode.

The decline of Babylon was also intertwined with geopolitical changes in the region. The Hittites, an emerging power in Anatolia, challenged Babylon's dominance and launched military campaigns to expand their own territories. This confrontation weakened Babylon's position and contributed to a gradual loss of control over the empire's outer regions.

Furthermore, the Assyrians, a formidable military force from the north, started to assert their influence and encroach upon Babylonian territories. The Assyrians, known for their ruthless tactics and advanced military strategies, posed a significant threat to the stability of the empire.

Amidst these external pressures, internal strife and political instability plagued Babylon. Successive rulers struggled to assert their authority and maintain the loyalty of their subjects. Corruption, rebellions, and palace intrigues weakened the fabric of Babylonian society, further hastening the decline of the empire.

Culturally, Babylon continued to be a center of intellectual and artistic achievements, but the tumultuous political climate took its toll on the empire's ability to govern effectively. The legacy of Hammurabi's Code endured, serving as a legal reference for generations to come, but the empire's once-grand vision of justice and unity began to fade.

Chapter 3 delves into the shadows of power that loomed over the Babylonian Empire. It explores the internal conflicts, external threats, and geopolitical changes that contributed to the decline of the empire. The chapter sheds light on the challenges faced by subsequent rulers, the rise of rival powers, and the erosion of centralized governance. It paints a picture of a once-mighty empire grappling with its own internal divisions and external pressures, foreshadowing the ultimate fall of Babylon.

Chapter 4: The Enigmatic Maya Civilization

Deep within the lush jungles of Mesoamerica, a civilization flourished in splendid isolation, leaving behind a legacy of breathtaking architectural marvels, sophisticated astronomical knowledge, and a vibrant cultural tapestry. Chapter 4 unravels the enigmatic world of the Maya civilization, shedding light on their fascinating history, achievements, and the mysteries that still captivate researchers today.

The Maya civilization emerged around 2000 BCE in the tropical lowlands of present-day Mexico, Guatemala, Belize, and Honduras. Their society was characterized by city-states, each with its own ruling elite and a complex system of governance. The Maya excelled in various fields, including agriculture, architecture, mathematics, and astronomy, creating a civilization that was both intellectually advanced and spiritually rich.

One of the most remarkable aspects of Maya civilization was their architectural prowess. The Maya built awe-inspiring cities with monumental structures, such as temples, pyramids, palaces, and ball courts. These structures showcased their intricate knowledge of engineering, precise measurements, and sophisticated construction techniques. The most iconic Maya site, Chichen Itza, with its monumental pyramid known as El Castillo, stands as a testament to their architectural brilliance and astronomical alignment.

The Maya also possessed an advanced understanding of astronomy. They meticulously observed the movements of celestial bodies, developed accurate calendars, and used their astronomical knowledge to guide agricultural practices and religious rituals. Their celestial observations were reflected in their architecture, with structures aligned to capture significant astronomical events, such as solstices and equinoxes.

The Maya had a complex system of hieroglyphic writing, known as Maya script, which enabled them to record historical events, religious ceremonies, and astronomical observations. Their codices, bark-paper books, contained a wealth of knowledge and served as repositories of their culture and history. Although many of these codices were destroyed during the Spanish conquest, several rare surviving examples provide glimpses into the rich intellectual and artistic tradition of the Maya.

Trade played a crucial role in Maya society, connecting different city-states and facilitating the exchange of goods, ideas, and cultural practices. The Maya established extensive trade networks, traversing the diverse landscapes of Mesoamerica. They traded commodities such as jade, obsidian, cacao, feathers, and textiles, fostering economic prosperity and cultural exchange across the region.

Despite their accomplishments, the Maya civilization experienced periods of conflict, political rivalries, and territorial disputes. City-states vied for power and influence, leading to intermittent warfare. However, the Maya also forged alliances and engaged in diplomatic exchanges, showcasing their diplomatic acumen and negotiation skills.

Throughout the chapter, the enigmatic nature of the Maya civilization becomes apparent. The reasons behind the decline of the Maya civilization remain a subject of debate among scholars. Factors such as environmental degradation, overpopulation, warfare, and socio-political upheaval have been proposed as contributing factors. Nevertheless, the enduring mysteries surrounding the collapse of Maya cities and the abandonment of once-thriving urban centers continue to captivate the imagination of researchers and historians.

Chapter 4 unveils the captivating world of the Maya civilization, delving into their architectural achievements, astronomical knowledge, hieroglyphic writing, and vibrant trade networks. It also acknowledges the challenges and complexities faced by Maya society, highlighting their resilience, cultural richness, and the enduring allure of their civilization. The Maya civilization's enigmatic legacy continues to fascinate and inspire, reminding us of the profound intellectual and artistic achievements of ancient Mesoamerica.

Chapter 5: The Golden Age of Greece

In the annals of history, ancient Greece shines as a beacon of intellectual, artistic, and political brilliance. Chapter 5 unravels the golden age of Greece, a time of unprecedented cultural achievements, philosophical inquiry, and democratic ideals.

The golden age of Greece is commonly associated with the 5th century BCE, a period known as the Classical period. During this time, the city-state of Athens emerged as a center of intellectual and artistic excellence, captivating the world with its democratic ideals and cultural contributions.

At the heart of Athens' golden age was the birth of democracy. The Athenian democracy, though limited in its scope, allowed citizens to participate in the decision-making process, fostering a sense of civic duty and collective responsibility. This democratic experiment laid the foundation for the development of political philosophy and inspired future generations to strive for self-governance.

In the realm of philosophy, ancient Greece produced some of the greatest thinkers in history. Socrates, Plato, and Aristotle embarked on a quest for knowledge, exploring fundamental questions about the nature of existence, ethics, and governance. Their philosophical dialogues and teachings continue to shape intellectual discourse to this day, influencing fields as diverse as ethics, metaphysics, and political theory.

The golden age of Greece also witnessed remarkable artistic achievements. Architecture reached new heights with the construction of magnificent temples, including the Parthenon atop the Acropolis. Sculpture flourished, with artists like Phidias producing iconic masterpieces such as the statue of Athena Parthenos. Drama thrived, with playwrights like Aeschylus, Sophocles, and Euripides crafting timeless tragedies and comedies that explored the depths of human emotion and moral dilemmas.

The spirit of inquiry extended to the sciences as well. Ancient Greek mathematicians, such as Euclid and Pythagoras, made significant contributions to geometry and number theory. The medical traditions of Hippocrates laid the groundwork for rational and empirical approaches to medicine that are still relevant today. Greece became a hub of intellectual exchange, with scholars and philosophers from across the Mediterranean converging in Athens to engage in dialogue, debate, and the pursuit of knowledge.

The golden age of Greece, however, was not without its challenges. The Peloponnesian War, fought between Athens and Sparta, brought about a decline in Athenian power and marked the beginning of a gradual decline for the Greek city-states as a whole. Internal conflicts, shifting alliances, and external invasions further weakened the once-thriving Greek civilization.

Yet, the legacy of Greece endured. The achievements of this golden age laid the groundwork for Western civilization and shaped the course of human history. The ideals of democracy, the pursuit of knowledge, and the celebration of human creativity and expression continue to resonate with societies around the world.

Chapter 5 delves into the golden age of Greece, exploring the birth of democracy, the flourishing of philosophy and the arts, and the enduring impact of ancient Greek achievements. It recognizes the challenges faced by the Greek city-states, but also highlights the enduring legacy of their cultural and intellectual contributions. The golden age of Greece stands as a testament to the heights that human civilization can reach when nurtured by the pursuit of knowledge, freedom of thought, and the expression of human creativity.

Chapter 6: The Roman Empire Ascendant

In the expansive realms of the ancient Mediterranean, a powerful empire emerged, destined to shape the course of history for centuries to come. Chapter 6 delves into the rise of the Roman Empire, its conquests, and the establishment of a vast imperial domain that left an indelible mark on the world.

The story of the Roman Empire begins with the city-state of Rome itself. Originally a humble settlement nestled along the banks of the Tiber River, Rome gradually expanded its influence, absorbing neighboring territories and establishing itself as a dominant power in the region.

Under the leadership of skilled military commanders and astute statesmen, Rome embarked on a series of conquests, gradually expanding its borders to encompass vast territories stretching from Britain in the northwest to the Euphrates River in the east. The Roman legions, disciplined and battle-hardened, swept across the known world, leaving a trail of conquered nations and assimilated cultures in their wake.

The success of the Roman Empire can be attributed to various factors. Its military prowess, marked by effective strategies, advanced weaponry, and a well-organized command structure, allowed Rome to overcome formidable adversaries. The Roman army's ability to integrate and assimilate conquered peoples into its ranks also contributed to its strength and stability.

Roman governance was characterized by a unique blend of centralized authority and local administration. The empire was divided into provinces, each overseen by a governor appointed by Rome. This system allowed for the efficient collection of taxes, the maintenance of order, and the dissemination of Roman culture and values throughout the empire.

Roman society was marked by a diverse array of cultures, religions, and traditions. As the empire expanded, it absorbed and assimilated various customs and beliefs, creating a rich tapestry of cultural exchange. Roman law, administration, and engineering prowess left an enduring impact on conquered lands, shaping their infrastructure, legal systems, and governance for centuries to come.

The Pax Romana, or Roman Peace, was a period of relative stability and prosperity that spanned over two centuries. During this time, trade flourished, roads were constructed, and cities thrived. The Roman Empire became a melting pot of cultures, fostering the exchange of ideas, goods, and innovations across its vast expanse.

Yet, the story of the Roman Empire was not without its challenges. Internal conflicts, power struggles, and political intrigues often threatened the stability of the empire. Economic disparities, class divisions, and the strains of governing such a vast domain posed constant challenges to Roman authority.

Chapter 6 unravels the ascendance of the Roman Empire, exploring its conquests, governance, and cultural influence. It delves into the military might of Rome, the assimilation of conquered territories, and the establishment of an empire that would endure for centuries. It acknowledges the complexities and challenges faced by Rome, but also highlights its remarkable achievements and enduring legacy. The Roman Empire stands as a testament to the heights of human ambition, the complexities of governance, and the profound impact that an empire can have on the world.

Chapter 7: The Age of Exploration and Discovery

In the annals of human history, the Age of Exploration stands as a testament to the insatiable curiosity and indomitable spirit of discovery. Chapter 7 delves into this transformative era, when intrepid explorers set sail across uncharted seas, braving the unknown in search of new lands, riches, and knowledge.

The Age of Exploration emerged in the 15th century, driven by a convergence of factors that ignited a fervor for exploration. Advances in shipbuilding technology, such as the development of the caravel and improved navigational instruments like the astrolabe and compass, enabled sailors to venture beyond familiar waters with greater confidence. Additionally, economic motivations, including the desire for new trade routes and access to valuable resources, fueled the ambitions of monarchs, merchants, and adventurers alike.

One of the pivotal figures of this era was Christopher Columbus, whose voyage in 1492 across the Atlantic Ocean heralded a new era of transoceanic exploration. Believing he had reached Asia, Columbus's journey instead led him to the Americas, forever altering the course of history and initiating a period of intense exploration and colonization.

The Spanish and Portuguese quickly followed in Columbus's wake, embarking on ambitious voyages of their own. Explorers such as Ferdinand Magellan, Vasco da Gama, and Hernán Cortés traversed the globe, mapping new territories, establishing trade networks, and encountering diverse cultures. Their expeditions opened up vast new possibilities, challenging existing beliefs about the world and expanding the known horizons of humanity.

The Age of Exploration was not without its controversies and hardships. The encounters between explorers and indigenous peoples often led to conflict, exploitation, and the imposition of foreign rule. The consequences of these interactions continue to shape the social, cultural, and political landscapes of the present day.

Nevertheless, the Age of Exploration also brought about immense cultural exchange, scientific discoveries, and the sharing of knowledge. It introduced Europeans to the wonders of the New World, unveiling exotic flora and fauna, and sparking a renewed interest in natural sciences. The exploration of distant lands inspired literary works, artistic masterpieces, and a reimagining of the world as Europeans grappled with the vastness and diversity of their newfound discoveries.

Chapter 7 explores the Age of Exploration in all its complexity and grandeur. It recounts the adventures of notable explorers, the challenges they faced, and the profound impact their voyages had on global history. It examines the motivations behind exploration, the clash of cultures, and the enduring legacy of this transformative era.

The Age of Exploration marked a turning point in human history, forever expanding the boundaries of knowledge, reshaping global trade and power dynamics, and laying the foundation for a truly interconnected world. It stands as a testament to the indomitable spirit of human curiosity and the remarkable achievements that can arise from the audacity to explore the unknown.

Chapter 8: The Industrial Revolution: A World Transformed

The 18th and 19th centuries witnessed a profound transformation in human society and the way people lived and worked. This chapter delves into the Industrial Revolution, a period of unprecedented technological advancements, economic growth, and social change that reshaped the world as we know it.

The Industrial Revolution began in Great Britain in the late 18th century and soon spread to other parts of Europe and North America. It marked a shift from an agrarian and craft-based economy to one dominated by mechanized manufacturing and industrial production. This period was characterized by the invention and implementation of new technologies, such as the steam engine, textile machinery, and iron and steel production techniques.

The steam engine, invented by James Watt, was a game-changer that revolutionized transportation, manufacturing, and agriculture. It powered locomotives, steamships, and factories, enabling the efficient movement of goods and people on an unprecedented scale. The textile industry also experienced a significant transformation with the introduction of mechanized spinning and weaving machines, such as the spinning jenny and the power loom. These innovations increased productivity and output, leading to the growth of factory-based textile production.

The impact of the Industrial Revolution was not limited to the realm of manufacturing. It brought about profound changes in society, culture, and the organization of labor. As factories sprouted across the landscape, rural communities transformed into bustling industrial towns and cities. The mass migration of people from rural areas to urban centers resulted in overcrowded and unsanitary living conditions, giving rise to social and health challenges.

The Industrial Revolution also had far-reaching consequences for the working class. Workers, including men, women, and children, found themselves laboring long hours in dangerous conditions for low wages. The rise of factories and mechanized production reduced the need for skilled craftsmen, leading to a decline in traditional artisanal trades.

Nevertheless, the Industrial Revolution brought about significant advancements in living standards, technology, and economic growth. It fueled the expansion of global trade, the development of infrastructure, and the accumulation of wealth. The emergence of the middle class and the growth of consumerism reshaped social dynamics and transformed patterns of consumption.

Chapter 8 delves into the complexities and implications of the Industrial Revolution. It examines the technological innovations that sparked this revolution, the social and economic impact on different segments of society, and the long-term consequences for human progress. The Industrial Revolution stands as a pivotal moment in history, marking the transition to a modern industrialized world and setting the stage for further advancements in science, technology, and social reform.

While the Industrial Revolution brought about significant progress and prosperity, it also exposed the inherent challenges and inequalities of rapid industrialization. The repercussions of this transformative era continue to be felt to this day, shaping our understanding of labor rights, environmental sustainability, and the balance between technological advancement and social welfare.

Chapter 9: The World Wars: A Global Upheaval

The 20th century was marked by two devastating world wars that reshaped the geopolitical landscape and inflicted immeasurable human suffering. Chapter 9 delves into the causes, events, and consequences of these global conflicts, exploring the political tensions, military strategies, and the profound impact on societies around the world.

The seeds of the First World War were sown in the complex web of alliances, rivalries, and competing interests among European powers. The assassination of Archduke Franz Ferdinand of Austria-Hungary in 1914 served as the spark that ignited the flames of war. The conflict quickly escalated, drawing in nations from across the globe and engulfing the world in a devastating conflict.

The First World War was characterized by trench warfare, technological advancements in weaponry, and staggering casualties. It saw the use of tanks, aircraft, and chemical weapons, transforming the nature of warfare and inflicting immense human suffering. The war drew to a close in 1918, leaving behind a legacy of political upheaval, the redrawing of national borders, and the seeds of future conflicts.

In the aftermath of the First World War, the world struggled to find stability and lasting peace. The Treaty of Versailles, signed in 1919, imposed harsh penalties on Germany and laid the groundwork for simmering resentment and a desire for revenge. Economic hardships, social unrest, and the rise of nationalist movements set the stage for the Second World War.

The Second World War, which erupted in 1939, witnessed the emergence of new military strategies, such as blitzkrieg warfare and the use of advanced weaponry. It engulfed the world once again, with major powers including Germany, Italy, Japan, and the Allied forces locked in a global struggle for dominance.

The horrors of the Holocaust, the devastation of cities through bombings, and the untold human suffering during this period serve as stark reminders of the consequences of unchecked aggression and intolerance. The Second World War concluded in 1945 with the use of atomic bombs on Hiroshima and Nagasaki, leaving the world forever changed.

The world wars had far-reaching consequences that extended beyond the battlefield. They reshaped the balance of power among nations, accelerated technological advancements, and ushered in a new era of global interconnectedness. The establishment of international organizations such as the United Nations aimed to prevent future conflicts and promote cooperation among nations.

Chapter 9 delves into the complexities of the world wars, exploring the political ideologies, military strategies, and the enduring impact on societies and individuals. It examines the profound consequences of these conflicts, from the redrawing of national boundaries to the emergence of new political and economic systems.

The world wars are a somber reminder of the destructive capabilities of human conflict, but they also highlight the resilience and determination of individuals and nations in the face of adversity. The lessons learned from these conflicts continue to shape international relations, peacekeeping efforts, and our understanding of the need for diplomacy, cooperation, and the pursuit of peaceful resolutions to global conflicts.

Chapter 10: The Space Age: Humanity Reaches for the Stars

The exploration of space stands as one of the most remarkable achievements in human history. Chapter 10 delves into the Space Age, a period of scientific discovery, technological advancements, and unprecedented human endeavors as humanity reached beyond the confines of Earth and ventured into the vastness of space.

The Space Age began in the mid-20th century, fueled by the intense competition between the United States and the Soviet Union during the Cold War. The launch of the Soviet satellite Sputnik in 1957 marked the dawn of the space race, igniting a fervor of scientific exploration and technological innovation.

The race to conquer space reached its climax with the Apollo program of the United States. In 1969, the Apollo 11 mission successfully landed astronauts Neil Armstrong and Buzz Aldrin on the lunar surface, making them the first humans to set foot on another celestial body. This monumental achievement captivated the world, symbolizing the triumph of human ingenuity and the realization of a seemingly impossible dream.

The exploration of space expanded our understanding of the universe, revolutionized communication, and paved the way for numerous technological advancements. Satellites, such as those used for telecommunications, weather monitoring, and navigation systems, now orbit the Earth, enabling global connectivity and enhancing our daily lives.

Beyond Earth's orbit, space probes and telescopes have provided us with invaluable insights into the cosmos. Robotic explorers, such as the Voyager spacecraft, have ventured to the outer reaches of our solar system, capturing stunning images and collecting data that have expanded our knowledge of distant planets, moons, and celestial phenomena.

The International Space Station (ISS), a collaboration between multiple nations, has served as a testament to the potential of international cooperation in space exploration. It has fostered scientific research, technological innovation, and a deeper understanding of the physiological and psychological challenges of long-duration space travel.

The Space Age has not been without its challenges and tragedies. The loss of lives, such as the Apollo 1 crew and the Challenger and Columbia space shuttle disasters, serves as a poignant reminder of the risks involved in space exploration. However, these setbacks have spurred advancements in safety measures and a renewed commitment to pushing the boundaries of human exploration.

Chapter 10 explores the triumphs and setbacks of the Space Age, the scientific discoveries, and the technological breakthroughs that have propelled humanity's journey beyond Earth. It delves into the challenges of living and working in space, the collaborative efforts among nations, and the ongoing pursuit of new frontiers.

The exploration of space represents the inherent human desire to push boundaries, expand our knowledge, and strive for new horizons. It inspires awe and wonder, reminding us of the vastness of the universe and our place within it. The Space Age serves as a testament to our collective imagination, innovation, and the indomitable spirit of exploration that defines our species.

Chapter 11: The Digital Revolution: Transforming the Information Age

The rapid advancement of technology in the late 20th and early 21st centuries ushered in the Digital Revolution, a period of profound transformation in how we create, share, and access information. Chapter 11 delves into this revolution, exploring the emergence of digital technologies, their impact on society, and the ongoing evolution of the Information Age.

The Digital Revolution was fueled by the development of computers, the internet, and digital communication technologies. The invention of the microprocessor, the miniaturization of computer components, and the creation of user-friendly interfaces made computing accessible to a wider audience. Computers evolved from room-sized machines to sleek, portable devices that fit in the palm of our hands.

The internet emerged as a global network, connecting people and information across vast distances. It revolutionized communication, enabling real-time interactions, instant access to knowledge, and the creation of virtual communities. The World Wide Web, introduced by Sir Tim Berners-Lee in the late 1980s, provided a user-friendly interface for navigating and sharing information online.

The Digital Revolution transformed various aspects of society. It revolutionized the way we work, with the automation of tasks, the rise of remote work, and the proliferation of digital platforms. It transformed the entertainment industry, with the advent of streaming services, digital music, and online gaming. It revolutionized commerce, with the rise of e-commerce, online marketplaces, and digital payment systems.

Social media platforms emerged as powerful tools for communication, networking, and self-expression. They reshaped the way we connect with others, share our thoughts and experiences, and consume news and information. However, they also raised concerns about privacy, digital surveillance, and the spread of misinformation.

The Digital Revolution gave rise to transformative innovations in various fields. Artificial intelligence and machine learning revolutionized data analysis, automation, and decision-making processes. Virtual reality and augmented reality technologies provided immersive experiences in entertainment, gaming, and education. The Internet of Things interconnected devices, enabling smart homes, wearable technology, and greater automation in various industries.

Chapter 11 delves into the multifaceted impact of the Digital Revolution. It examines the opportunities and challenges presented by digital technologies, including issues of privacy, cybersecurity, and digital divide. It explores the evolving landscape of media and communication, the influence of social media, and the changing nature of work and commerce.

The Digital Revolution continues to evolve at an unprecedented pace, with new technologies and innovations shaping our daily lives. It holds immense potential for positive change, but also poses ethical dilemmas and societal challenges. As we navigate this digital landscape, it becomes increasingly crucial to foster digital literacy, responsible technology use, and to ensure equitable access to the benefits of the digital age.

The Digital Revolution is an ongoing journey, a testament to human ingenuity and our ability to harness technology for the betterment of society. It has transformed the way we live, work, and connect, fundamentally reshaping the fabric of our existence in the Information Age.

Chapter 12: The Age of Sustainability: Nurturing a Greener Future

As the world grapples with the challenges of climate change, resource depletion, and environmental degradation, a new era has emerged—the Age of Sustainability. Chapter 12 delves into this critical shift, exploring the growing awareness of our planet's fragility, the adoption of sustainable practices, and the collective efforts to forge a greener and more sustainable future.

The Age of Sustainability is characterized by a fundamental shift in our understanding of our relationship with the environment. It recognizes the interdependence of ecological systems and human well-being, emphasizing the need for responsible stewardship of natural resources and the preservation of biodiversity.

One of the key drivers of sustainability is the recognition of climate change as a global crisis. The scientific consensus on the role of human activities in altering the Earth's climate has spurred widespread action. Governments, organizations, and individuals are now working to reduce greenhouse gas emissions, transition to renewable energy sources, and develop sustainable practices in various sectors.

The adoption of sustainable practices extends beyond energy and climate. It encompasses sustainable agriculture, responsible consumption and production, waste reduction and recycling, and the protection of ecosystems and biodiversity. Sustainable development aims to meet present needs without compromising the ability of future generations to meet their own needs.

The Age of Sustainability also recognizes the importance of social equity and justice. It emphasizes the need for inclusive and fair systems that address inequality, promote social well-being, and ensure access to basic needs and opportunities for all. Sustainability is not only about environmental considerations but also encompasses social and economic dimensions.

Numerous initiatives and movements have emerged to drive the sustainability agenda forward. Organizations and businesses are implementing sustainable practices, adopting circular economy models, and pursuing environmentally friendly innovations. Grassroots movements, youth activism, and public awareness campaigns are mobilizing communities and pushing for systemic change.

Chapter 12 explores the various facets of the Age of Sustainability. It examines the role of renewable energy, the importance of sustainable urban planning, the need for responsible consumption and waste management, and the challenges and opportunities in achieving a sustainable future.

While the challenges ahead are immense, the Age of Sustainability offers hope and possibilities. It calls for collaboration, innovation, and a collective commitment to address the pressing environmental and social issues of our time. By embracing sustainable practices, nurturing a respect for nature, and prioritizing the well-being of both present and future generations, we can shape a greener, more resilient, and harmonious world.

The Age of Sustainability is an invitation to reimagine our relationship with the planet and adopt a mindset of stewardship and responsibility. It is a call to action to align our actions, policies, and aspirations with the principles of sustainability, in pursuit of a future where humanity thrives in harmony with nature.

Chapter 13: The Age of Connectivity: Uniting a Global Society

The world has become increasingly interconnected, with technological advancements and global communication networks bridging distances and bringing people closer than ever before. Chapter 13 delves into the Age of Connectivity, exploring the profound impact of technology on society, the transformation of communication, and the emergence of a truly globalized world.

The Age of Connectivity is characterized by the proliferation of digital communication technologies, enabling instantaneous and widespread connections across the globe. The advent of the internet, mobile devices, and social media platforms has revolutionized the way we interact, share information, and engage in a global dialogue.

The internet has transformed communication, breaking down barriers of time and space. Instant messaging, video calls, and social media platforms allow individuals to connect with friends, family, and colleagues regardless of geographical distance. Online communities and social networks provide spaces for like-minded individuals to come together, share ideas, and collaborate on a global scale.

The Age of Connectivity has also witnessed the rise of e-commerce and digital marketplaces, enabling consumers to access products and services from around the world with a few clicks. This interconnectedness has facilitated global trade, opening up new opportunities for businesses and consumers alike.

Education and learning have also been greatly impacted by connectivity. Online courses, e-learning platforms, and digital resources have made education more accessible, allowing individuals to acquire knowledge and skills from anywhere in the world. The Age of Connectivity has democratized education, breaking down barriers to learning and fostering a lifelong pursuit of knowledge.

The global reach of connectivity has had a profound impact on culture and the arts. People from different backgrounds and cultures can now share their stories, traditions, and artistic expressions with a global audience. Online platforms have given rise to a diverse range of digital content, including music, films, and literature, transcending geographical boundaries and enriching our cultural experiences.

However, the Age of Connectivity is not without its challenges. The rapid dissemination of information has led to an abundance of news sources, making it increasingly important to navigate through a sea of information and discern credible sources. Concerns over privacy, cybersecurity, and the digital divide also pose challenges as we strive to ensure equitable access to connectivity and safeguard individuals' rights in the digital realm.

Chapter 13 explores the multifaceted impact of the Age of Connectivity, examining the social, economic, and cultural transformations brought about by technological advancements. It delves into the opportunities and challenges presented by this interconnected world, the importance of digital literacy, and the need for ethical and responsible use of technology.

The Age of Connectivity offers immense potential for collaboration, innovation, and the exchange of ideas. It allows us to transcend geographical and cultural boundaries, fostering a global society where diverse voices are heard and interconnectedness is celebrated. By harnessing the power of connectivity responsibly and inclusively, we can build a future where everyone has the opportunity to connect, share, and contribute to a more united and understanding world.

As we navigate the complexities of the Age of Connectivity, it becomes crucial to strike a balance between virtual interactions and the preservation of meaningful human connections. The true value of connectivity lies not only in the technology itself but in our ability to use it as a tool for empathy, understanding, and positive change.

Chapter 14: The Quest for Knowledge: Exploring the Frontiers of Science and Discovery

Humanity has always been driven by curiosity and a desire to uncover the mysteries of the universe. Chapter 14 delves into the Quest for Knowledge, exploring the relentless pursuit of scientific understanding, the breakthroughs that have shaped our world, and the boundless frontiers of discovery that lie ahead.

Science is the cornerstone of human progress, fueling innovation, advancements in technology, and our understanding of the natural world. It encompasses a wide range of disciplines, from physics and chemistry to biology and astronomy, each contributing to our collective knowledge and pushing the boundaries of what we know.

Throughout history, scientific discoveries have revolutionized our understanding of the universe. From the groundbreaking theories of Isaac Newton and Albert Einstein to the discovery of the structure of DNA by James Watson and Francis Crick, these moments of insight have reshaped our understanding of ourselves and the world we inhabit.

The Quest for Knowledge is not limited to any single field of study but spans the entire spectrum of human curiosity. It includes the exploration of outer space, the depths of the oceans, the mysteries of the human brain, and the intricacies of the microscopic world. Each frontier presents its unique challenges and opportunities for exploration.

Advancements in technology have been instrumental in unlocking the secrets of the universe. Powerful telescopes have allowed us to peer deeper into space, revealing distant galaxies and unraveling the origins of the cosmos. Microscopes have enabled us to delve into the intricate world of cells and molecules, unraveling the building blocks of life.

Scientific inquiry also extends beyond the confines of academia and research institutions. Citizen science initiatives and collaborative projects involve people from all walks of life in the process of discovery. This democratization of knowledge allows individuals to contribute to scientific research and expand the frontiers of human understanding.

The Quest for Knowledge is driven by a sense of wonder and a deep desire to unravel the mysteries of existence. It is a testament to human curiosity and our innate need to make sense of the world around us. With each discovery, we gain new insights and raise new questions, propelling us further along the path of knowledge.

Chapter 14 explores the vast expanse of scientific exploration, highlighting key discoveries, breakthroughs, and the individuals who have shaped our understanding of the world. It delves into the methods and principles of scientific inquiry, the importance of collaboration and interdisciplinary approaches, and the ethical considerations that come with scientific advancements.

As we venture into the unknown, the Quest for Knowledge reminds us of the importance of critical thinking, intellectual curiosity, and an open-minded approach. It encourages us to embrace the wonders of the natural world, to question the limits of our current understanding, and to pursue scientific endeavors with a sense of awe and humility.

The Quest for Knowledge is an ongoing journey, a testament to the power of human curiosity and the unrelenting pursuit of truth. It is a journey that transcends borders and cultures, uniting us in our shared quest to unlock the secrets of the universe and leave a lasting legacy of understanding for future generations.

Chapter 15: The Human Spirit: Resilience, Hope, and the Power of Change

In the face of adversity and challenges, the human spirit has demonstrated remarkable resilience, unwavering hope, and the power to instigate change. Chapter 15 explores the depths of the human spirit, showcasing inspiring stories of courage, perseverance, and the transformative impact individuals can have on the world.

Throughout history, humanity has faced countless trials, from wars and conflicts to natural disasters and pandemics. Yet, in the face of these hardships, individuals and communities have displayed remarkable strength, banding together to rebuild, heal, and create a better future.

Resilience is a fundamental characteristic of the human spirit. It is the ability to adapt, bounce back from adversity, and find strength in the face of challenges. From survivors of natural disasters who rebuild their lives from the ground up to individuals overcoming personal struggles and rising above limitations, the human spirit has shown an indomitable will to thrive.

Hope is another powerful force that drives the human spirit. It is the belief in the possibility of a better tomorrow, even in the darkest of times. Hope inspires individuals to dream, to envision a brighter future, and to work towards making that vision a reality. It fuels optimism, fuels action, and fuels the pursuit of change.

The human spirit is also a catalyst for change. Throughout history, individuals have emerged as agents of transformation, challenging the status quo, and advocating for social justice, equality, and human rights. From civil rights leaders like Martin Luther King Jr. to environmental activists like Greta Thunberg, these individuals have harnessed the power of their convictions to ignite movements and bring about systemic change.

Chapter 15 weaves together stories of resilience, hope, and transformative change. It highlights the triumph of the human spirit in the face of adversity, showcasing individuals who have overcome personal struggles, defied societal norms, and made a lasting impact on the world. These stories serve as a testament to the power of the individual and the profound difference one person can make.

The human spirit reminds us of our shared humanity, the interconnectedness of our experiences, and our capacity to support and uplift one another. It is a reminder that even in the face of daunting challenges, there is always room for growth, healing, and positive change.

As we navigate the complexities of the modern world, the stories of resilience, hope, and transformative change serve as beacons of inspiration. They remind us of the strength that resides within each of us and the potential we have to shape a better future for ourselves and generations to come.

The human spirit is a testament to the indomitable nature of the human will. It is a call to action, urging us to tap into our inner strength, embrace hope, and become catalysts for positive change in our communities and the world at large.

Chapter 15 concludes the book, leaving readers with a sense of awe and admiration for the resilience, hope, and transformative power of the human spirit. It serves as a reminder that no matter the challenges we face, the human spirit is an enduring force that can guide us towards a brighter, more compassionate, and inclusive future.

Epilogue: Embracing the Tapestry of Humanity: A Call to Unity and Understanding

The Rise & Fall of Ancient Civilizations and the False Matrix has taken us on a journey through the annals of history, exploring the rise and decline of powerful empires, unraveling the webs of deception woven by the False Matrix, and delving into the enduring strength of the human spirit. As we reach the end of this captivating narrative, the epilogue invites us to reflect on the lessons learned and embrace the tapestry of humanity with unity and understanding.

Throughout the book, we have witnessed the rise and fall of ancient civilizations, each with its unique contributions and legacies. From the grandeur of Egypt's pyramids to the philosophical wisdom of ancient Greece, these civilizations have left an indelible mark on human history. They remind us of the impermanence of power and the importance of collective memory in preserving our shared heritage.

Simultaneously, we have explored the concept of the False Matrix, a metaphorical construct that represents the illusions and falsehoods that can pervade societies and individuals. It serves as a reminder of the dangers of misinformation, manipulation, and the importance of critical thinking. By unraveling the layers of the False Matrix, we empower ourselves to seek truth, question narratives, and navigate a complex world with discernment.

As we reflect on the rise and fall of civilizations and the deceptions of the False Matrix, it becomes evident that the human experience is a tapestry woven with threads of diversity. Our world is a mosaic of cultures, beliefs, and perspectives, each contributing to the richness and complexity of our shared existence. It is in embracing this tapestry that we can truly foster unity and understanding.

The epilogue calls upon us to transcend the divisions that often separate us – be they political, religious, or cultural – and embrace the common threads that bind us together. It is through dialogue, empathy, and an openness to different perspectives that we can bridge divides and build a more inclusive and harmonious world.

In the tapestry of humanity, every thread has value. Each person, regardless of their background or beliefs, carries a unique perspective and contribution to offer. By embracing diversity and actively seeking to understand one another, we create a fertile ground for collaboration, growth, and mutual respect.

The journey through the pages of this book has been one of exploration, discovery, and reflection. It has allowed us to delve into the mysteries of ancient civilizations, question the narratives that shape our perception, and celebrate the resilience and transformative power of the human spirit. Now, as we close this chapter, we are called upon to carry the lessons learned and the spirit of unity forward into our own lives.

The Rise & Fall of Ancient Civilizations and the False Matrix invites us to be active participants in shaping our collective destiny. It urges us to rise above the illusions of division, to challenge oppressive systems, and to cultivate empathy and compassion in our interactions with others. It is a call to action, inspiring us to create a world where the lessons of the past guide us towards a brighter future.

In embracing the tapestry of humanity, we honor the ancient civilizations that have come before us, we reject the falsehoods that seek to divide us, and we pave the way for a world where unity, understanding, and shared prosperity flourish.

As the final chapter of this book closes, may it serve as a catalyst for personal reflection, meaningful conversations, and positive change. Let us embark on a journey of continued growth, embracing the tapestry of humanity with open hearts and minds, and forging a future that celebrates our shared humanity. Extra Bonus Piece: The Anunnaki

In the realm of ancient myths and legends, one intriguing and enigmatic group of beings that often captures the imagination is the Anunnaki. Originating from the ancient Mesopotamian region, the Anunnaki are believed to be a group of deities who played a significant role in the mythology and religious beliefs of the ancient civilizations of Sumer, Akkad, and Babylon.

According to Mesopotamian mythology, the Anunnaki were a pantheon of gods and goddesses who descended from the heavens to Earth. They were seen as the creators and shapers of human civilization, bestowing upon humanity the gifts of knowledge, technology, and cultural development. The term "Anunnaki" translates to "those who came from heaven to Earth" or "princely offspring" in the Sumerian language.

The Anunnaki were often depicted as divine beings of immense power and stature. In ancient artwork and texts, they were described as beings of great wisdom, possessing advanced knowledge of various sciences and arts. They were believed to possess the ability to manipulate the forces of nature and were associated with various aspects of human life, such as agriculture, fertility, justice, and warfare.

One of the most well-known stories involving the Anunnaki is the Epic of Gilgamesh, an ancient Mesopotamian epic poem. In this epic, the Anunnaki are portrayed as central figures, interacting with the hero Gilgamesh and influencing the course of his journey and adventures.

The exact nature and origin of the Anunnaki have been the subject of much speculation and debate. Some theories propose that they were extraterrestrial beings who visited Earth from another planet, bringing advanced knowledge and technology. Others interpret them as symbolic representations of natural forces or celestial bodies.

While the historical existence of the Anunnaki as actual deities is a matter of religious belief and interpretation, their enduring presence in ancient Mesopotamian mythology and their influence on subsequent cultures cannot be denied. The stories and legends surrounding the Anunnaki continue to captivate the imagination of people worldwide, fueling a fascination with ancient mysteries and alternative interpretations of human history.

Whether seen as gods, extraterrestrial beings, or mythical symbols, the Anunnaki remain an intriguing aspect of ancient civilizations. They serve as a reminder of the profound impact of mythology and religion on the development of human cultures and the enduring power of ancient legends to inspire curiosity and wonder.

Disclaimer: The existence and nature of the Anunnaki remain a topic of debate and interpretation, and the information presented here is based on historical and mythological sources. Different interpretations and beliefs exist, and readers are encouraged to explore various perspectives and draw their own conclusions.

The Anunnaki are often associated with the ancient Sumerian civilization, one of the earliest known civilizations in human history. Sumer was located in what is now southern Iraq and flourished around 4000 to 2000 BCE. The Sumerians believed that the Anunnaki were responsible for the creation of humanity and played a central role in their religious and cosmological beliefs.

According to Sumerian mythology, the Anunnaki were the children of Anu, the sky god, and his consort Ki, the earth goddess. They were considered divine beings who held immense power and authority. The Anunnaki were organized into a hierarchy, with Anu being the supreme ruler, and other deities serving various roles and responsibilities.

One of the well-known stories involving the Anunnaki is the Enuma Elish, the Babylonian creation myth. It tells the tale of how the god Marduk, an important deity in Babylonian mythology, emerged as the leader of the gods and defeated the primordial goddess Tiamat, bringing order to the cosmos. The Anunnaki are mentioned in this myth as the pantheon of gods who witnessed and participated in these events.

The role of the Anunnaki in Sumerian mythology extended beyond creation. They were believed to have a hand in shaping human destiny, granting kingship and establishing laws. Some texts suggest that they even intervened in human affairs, sometimes playing a part in wars and conflicts.

In later Babylonian and Assyrian mythology, the influence of the Anunnaki continued, although their significance may have changed. As the Mesopotamian civilizations evolved and different empires rose to power, the pantheon of gods underwent modifications and assimilated deities from other cultures, creating a complex and dynamic religious landscape.

It's important to note that while the Anunnaki were revered in ancient Mesopotamian religions, their existence as actual deities is a matter of religious belief and interpretation. Modern scholars analyze and interpret the texts and myths to understand the beliefs and worldview of ancient cultures, providing insights into the rich tapestry of human history and culture.

The fascination with the Anunnaki continues in modern times, with various alternative theories and speculations surrounding their true nature and influence. Some people interpret the Anunnaki as ancient astronauts or extraterrestrial beings who visited Earth in the distant past and influenced human development. These ideas have gained popularity in certain fringe circles and alternative historical narratives.

Ultimately, the Anunnaki remain an intriguing aspect of ancient Mesopotamian mythology and continue to spark curiosity and speculation about humanity's origins and the mysteries of our past. Their legacy endures as a testament to the enduring power of myth and the human quest for understanding the cosmos and our place within it.

The Anunnaki, as depicted in ancient Mesopotamian texts, were believed to have physical forms resembling humans but possessing godlike qualities and abilities. They were often portrayed as towering figures with extraordinary strength and knowledge. According to the myths, the Anunnaki possessed advanced technology and were credited with teaching humans various crafts, sciences, and spiritual knowledge.

One prominent figure among the Anunnaki is Enki, also known as Ea, who was considered the god of wisdom and the creator of mankind. Enki played a pivotal role in shaping human destiny and was associated with water, fertility, and the arts of civilization. His interactions with humans were often portrayed as benevolent and nurturing, guiding humanity towards progress and enlightenment.

Another significant Anunnaki deity is Enlil, the god of wind and storms. Enlil held a prominent position within the pantheon and was seen as a ruler and judge. He was responsible for maintaining order and enforcing divine laws, often depicted as a stern and authoritative figure.

The Anunnaki were not without their own conflicts and rivalries. Myths and texts describe power struggles and disputes among the gods, reflecting the complexities of human relationships and dynamics. These narratives often explored themes of ambition, jealousy, and the consequences of divine actions on human affairs.

While the Anunnaki are most closely associated with Sumerian mythology, their influence extended to neighboring civilizations as well. Babylonian, Assyrian, and Akkadian cultures adopted and integrated the Anunnaki pantheon into their own religious practices, although their specific roles and attributes may have varied.

The legacy of the Anunnaki continues to intrigue and inspire researchers, historians, and enthusiasts alike. Their stories and presence in ancient Mesopotamian mythology shed light on the beliefs, values, and aspirations of the people who lived in those times. They provide a glimpse into the complexities of ancient civilizations and their attempts to understand the forces at work in the world.

It's important to approach the study of the Anunnaki with a critical and open mind, considering both the historical context and the symbolic nature of mythological narratives. Interpretations of ancient texts and artifacts are subject to ongoing scholarly debate and revision, and new discoveries may shed further light on the role and significance of the Anunnaki in ancient Mesopotamian cultures.

The fascination with the Anunnaki and their potential connections to extraterrestrial beings or advanced ancient civilizations continues to captivate the imagination of many. However, it's essential to approach such speculative ideas with a balanced perspective, considering the available evidence and scholarly consensus.

In conclusion, the Anunnaki represent a fascinating aspect of ancient Mesopotamian mythology and offer insights into the religious beliefs, cultural values, and societal dynamics of the time. Exploring their stories and examining their influence allows us to delve into the depths of human imagination and the enduring allure of ancient mysteries.

The Anunnaki, with their prominent roles in ancient Mesopotamian mythology, continue to captivate the imagination and curiosity of people around the world. Whether seen as divine beings, symbolic representations, or even extraterrestrial entities, the Anunnaki hold a significant place in the tapestry of ancient civilizations.

Their stories and legends provide us with insights into the rich cultural heritage of Mesopotamia and the beliefs and aspirations of its people. From the creation of humanity to the bestowal of knowledge and the shaping of civilizations, the Anunnaki played a vital role in the religious and mythological narratives of ancient Mesopotamia.

While their existence as actual deities or extraterrestrial beings is a subject of debate and interpretation, the enduring allure of the Anunnaki lies in their capacity to inspire wonder, curiosity, and exploration. They serve as a reminder of the human quest for knowledge, the search for meaning, and the enduring power of myth and legend in shaping our understanding of the past.

As we delve into the mysteries of ancient civilizations, it is important to approach the study of the Anunnaki with an open mind, acknowledging the cultural context, historical perspectives, and the limitations of our knowledge. By exploring their stories and examining the evidence available, we gain a deeper appreciation for the diverse range of beliefs and mythologies that have shaped human cultures throughout history.

The fascination with the Anunnaki continues to drive ongoing research, speculative theories, and the quest for understanding. It is through the exploration of ancient myths, legends, and archaeological findings that we piece together fragments of the past, painting a more comprehensive picture of our shared human heritage.

In conclusion, the Anunnaki remain an intriguing and enigmatic aspect of ancient civilizations. They represent the enduring power of mythology and the human desire to comprehend our origins and the forces that shape our existence. Through their stories, we embark on a journey of discovery, unearthing the complexities of our past and unlocking the mysteries that still surround us.

As we continue to explore and uncover the secrets of ancient civilizations, the stories of the Anunnaki will undoubtedly continue to inspire, challenge, and fascinate us, inviting us to delve deeper into the realms of history, mythology, and the human spirit.

Ancient symbolism holds a profound significance in human history, spanning across various cultures and civilizations. Symbolism served as a means of communication, expressing complex ideas, beliefs, and emotions in a visual and often universal language. These symbols carried deep cultural and spiritual meanings, reflecting the worldview and values of the societies that employed them.

One of the most famous ancient symbols is the Egyptian Ankh, often referred to as the "Key of Life." This symbol, resembling a cross with a loop at the top, represented eternal life, regeneration, and the divine power of the gods. It was closely associated with the sun god Ra and was frequently depicted in Egyptian art and religious rituals.

In ancient Mesopotamia, the winged disk symbol, known as the Faravahar, held great importance in Zoroastrianism, the predominant religion of the Persian Empire. The Faravahar represented the eternal battle between good and evil, divine guidance, and the human quest for spiritual enlightenment. It depicted a winged figure, usually identified as the guardian spirit or Fravashi, hovering above a ring representing eternity.

The yin and yang symbol from ancient Chinese philosophy embodies the concept of dualism and harmony. It consists of two interconnected and complementary halves, one representing yin (feminine, passive, dark) and the other yang (masculine, active, light). The symbol signifies the balance and interdependence of opposites in the universe, such as light and dark, hot and cold, and chaos and order.

The Swastika, though controversial due to its association with Nazi Germany, has ancient roots and a different meaning in various cultures. Originally an auspicious symbol in Hinduism, Buddhism, and Jainism, it represents well-being, prosperity, and good fortune. It is a powerful example of how symbols can undergo profound transformations and acquire different connotations throughout history.

Another symbol that has transcended time and cultures is the Tree of Life. Found in many ancient mythologies and belief systems, including Norse, Celtic, and Mesopotamian, it symbolizes the interconnectedness of all living beings, the cycles of nature, and the continuity of life. The Tree of Life serves as a reminder of our connection to the natural world and our place within the larger cosmic order.

These are just a few examples of the vast array of ancient symbols and their meanings. Each culture and civilization developed its unique symbolism, often influenced by their environment, religious beliefs, and societal values. The study of ancient symbolism allows us to delve into the depths of human expression and understanding, providing insights into the universal themes and aspirations that have shaped our collective human experience.

Today, ancient symbols continue to resonate with people, offering a sense of connection to our shared human heritage and the timeless quest for meaning and transcendence. They serve as a reminder of the enduring power of visual language and the capacity of symbols to transcend language barriers and convey profound ideas and emotions.

As we explore the symbolism of ancient civilizations, we gain a deeper appreciation for the rich tapestry of human culture and the ways in which symbolism has shaped our understanding of the world. Ancient symbols carry with them a sense of mystery, inviting us to unravel their hidden meanings and contemplate the timeless wisdom they convey.

In conclusion, ancient symbolism is a testament to the creative and symbolic capacity of humanity. It speaks to our innate need for expression, connection, and understanding. By studying these symbols, we can uncover the depths of our shared human history and tap into the universal truths and aspirations that continue to resonate across time and cultures.

Who were the Sumerians?:

The Sumerians were an ancient civilization that existed in Mesopotamia, which is modern-day southern Iraq, around 4,500 to 1,900 BCE. They are considered one of the earliest urban societies in human history and are credited with significant contributions to the development of civilization.

The Sumerians built a number of city-states, with the city of Uruk being one of the most prominent. They developed a sophisticated system of writing known as cuneiform, which was one of the earliest known writing systems. Cuneiform was used to record various aspects of Sumerian life, including literature, laws, religious texts, and economic transactions.

The Sumerians made advancements in various fields, such as agriculture, architecture, mathematics, astronomy, and governance. They constructed impressive ziggurats (stepped pyramids) as religious structures and developed complex irrigation systems to support their agriculture. They also established a system of city-state governments, with each city having its own ruler.

Religion played a significant role in Sumerian society, with a pantheon of gods and goddesses worshipped by the people. The most prominent deities included Anu (the sky god), Enlil (the god of wind and storms), and Inanna (the goddess of love and war).

The Sumerians traded extensively with neighboring regions, which allowed them to acquire valuable resources. They also engaged in conflicts and warfare with other city-states, leading to power struggles and shifting alliances.

Over time, the Sumerians faced invasions and dominance by other civilizations, such as the Akkadians and Babylonians. The cultural and linguistic impact of the Sumerians, however, endured through subsequent Mesopotamian civilizations.

Today, the legacy of the Sumerians lives on through their contributions to literature, law, and various aspects of civilization. Their influence can be seen in the writings of later civilizations, such as the Babylonians and Assyrians, who built upon the foundations laid by the Sumerians.

Alien civilizations and the pyramids:

The idea that alien civilizations were involved in the construction of the pyramids is a popular topic in certain fringe theories and speculative discussions. However, it is important to note that there is no credible scientific evidence to support these claims. The mainstream scientific consensus is that the pyramids, such as the ones in Egypt, were built by ancient human civilizations.

The Egyptian pyramids, including the Great Pyramid of Giza, were constructed by the ancient Egyptians during the Old Kingdom period, specifically around 2,600 to 2,500 BCE. These impressive structures were built as monumental tombs for the pharaohs, who were the rulers of ancient Egypt.

The construction of the pyramids involved extensive planning, engineering, and labor. Ancient Egyptians had sophisticated architectural and engineering knowledge, along with a well-organized workforce consisting of skilled laborers and artisans. The pyramids were constructed using limestone blocks, which were quarried and transported to the construction sites.

The precise methods used by the ancient Egyptians to build the pyramids have been the subject of much study and research. Various theories propose that ramps, levers, and a combination of human effort and ingenuity were employed to move and position the massive stone blocks. Archaeological evidence, including ancient quarry sites, tools, and worker settlements, supports the understanding that the pyramids were built by human hands.

Claims suggesting alien involvement in pyramid construction often rely on misconceptions about the capabilities of ancient civilizations or underestimate the level of knowledge and skill possessed by ancient builders. The achievements of ancient civilizations, including the pyramids, can be understood within the context of human ingenuity, technological advancements, and the resources available to them at the time.

While the idea of alien civilizations and their potential influence on Earth is a captivating concept for science fiction and speculative discussions, it is important to differentiate between evidence-based historical knowledge and imaginative theories that lack scientific support.

Aliens and the Moon:

The topic of aliens and the moon has been the subject of various speculations, conspiracy theories, and science fiction stories. However, it is important to note that there is no credible scientific evidence to support the claim that aliens have visited or currently reside on the moon.

The moon is Earth's natural satellite, and it has been extensively studied by both robotic missions and human astronauts. Scientific exploration of the moon has provided valuable insights into its geology, origin, and the history of our solar system. The Apollo missions, conducted by NASA in the late 1960s and early 1970s, involved human landings on the moon and brought back lunar samples, which have been analyzed and studied by scientists.

The scientific consensus is that the moon is a barren, lifeless celestial body with no evidence of extraterrestrial life. The harsh environment of the moon, characterized by extreme temperatures, a lack of atmosphere, and intense radiation, makes it highly inhospitable for life as we know it. The absence of liquid water and organic compounds further diminishes the likelihood of life on the moon.

It is worth mentioning that some conspiracy theories suggest the existence of hidden alien bases or structures on the moon. However, these claims lack credible evidence and are generally considered to be unfounded. Images and data obtained from lunar missions conducted by various space agencies, including NASA, have been thoroughly analyzed and have not provided any substantiated evidence of alien activity.

While the moon continues to be a subject of scientific interest and exploration, the presence of aliens on the moon remains speculative and falls outside the realm of established scientific understanding. The focus of lunar exploration remains on advancing our knowledge of the moon's geology, its formation, and its potential for supporting future human missions.

The idea of being an original Annunaki descendant on Earth today is not supported by scientific evidence or mainstream scholarly consensus. The concept of Annunaki stems from ancient Mesopotamian mythology and refers to a group of deities in Sumerian and Babylonian cultures.

Claims of being a descendant of the Annunaki or possessing Annunaki DNA are typically associated with fringe theories and pseudoscience. It is important to approach such claims with skepticism and critical thinking, as they often lack credible evidence and rely on speculative interpretations of ancient texts.

While it is true that humans share a common ancestry and genetic heritage, tracing lineage specifically to the Annunaki is not a scientifically supported notion. Human evolutionary history and genetic studies provide insights into our origins as a species, highlighting our connections to other hominid species and the African continent.

It is crucial to differentiate between evidence-based scientific understanding and unfounded claims that can perpetuate misinformation and confusion. It is recommended to rely on reputable scientific sources and scholarly research when exploring topics related to human history, genetics, and mythology.

24 SIGNS THAT YOU COULD BE AN ORIGINAL ANNUNAKI DESCENDANT ON THE EARTH TODAY.

1. Annunaki believe that you can truly create something from nothing.

The belief that the Annunaki or any ancient civilization believed in creating something from nothing is not accurately supported by historical or mythological records. It's important to understand that ancient civilizations, including the Sumerians and Babylonians who referenced the Annunaki in their mythology, held different cosmological and creation beliefs.

In the mythologies of these civilizations, the creation of the world and existence of life were often attributed to the actions of gods or divine beings. However, these creation stories typically involved the transformation or organization of preexisting elements, rather than the creation of something from absolute nothingness.

For example, in the Babylonian creation myth known as the Enuma Elish, the world is said to have emerged through a series of events involving the separation and shaping of primeval elements like fresh water (Apsu) and saltwater (Tiamat). Similarly, in Sumerian mythology, the god Enki plays a role in shaping and organizing preexisting materials to create order in the world.

The concept of creating something from nothing is a complex philosophical and scientific question that extends beyond ancient mythologies. It is a topic that has been explored by thinkers in various fields, including philosophy, theology, and physics, but it remains a subject of ongoing debate and speculation.

In summary, the idea that the Annunaki or ancient civilizations believed in creating something from nothing is not an accurate representation of their cosmological beliefs as depicted in their mythologies and historical texts.

2. Annunaki are gifted in all of the powers to create matter from energy.

The notion that the Annunaki possessed the ability to create matter from energy is not supported by historical accounts, scientific evidence, or mainstream scholarly consensus. The concept of the Annunaki originates from ancient Mesopotamian mythologies and refers to a group of deities worshipped by the Sumerians and Babylonians.

In these mythologies, the Annunaki were associated with various aspects of human life, such as creation, kingship, and divine rule. However, there is no explicit mention or indication that they possessed the power to create matter from energy in ancient texts or historical records.

The ability to convert energy into matter, or vice versa, is a concept that falls within the domain of modern scientific understanding, particularly in the context of physics. It is explored in fields such as particle physics and nuclear reactions, where energy-matter conversion can occur under specific conditions. However, this process is highly complex and requires specialized equipment and controlled environments.

Claims attributing such powers to ancient beings like the Annunaki often arise from speculative or fictional sources that mix mythologies with modern concepts in an imaginative manner. It is important to approach these claims with critical thinking and rely on scientific knowledge and evidence-based understanding when exploring such topics.

In summary, the belief that the Annunaki possessed the ability to create matter from energy is not supported by historical sources or scientific consensus. The understanding of energy-matter conversion is a modern scientific concept that should be distinguished from ancient mythologies and their interpretations.

3. Annunaki hate all strict time schedules, especially being held to them.

The belief that the Annunaki had a disdain for strict time schedules is not supported by historical records or scholarly consensus. The Annunaki, as depicted in ancient Mesopotamian mythologies, were associated with various roles and responsibilities, including the governance of celestial bodies, the establishment of civilizations, and the granting of knowledge to humans.

While ancient mythologies often describe the Annunaki's interactions with humans and their involvement in shaping the world, there is no specific mention or indication that they held a particular aversion to time schedules or being bound by them.

Timekeeping and the establishment of calendars were crucial aspects of ancient civilizations, including those in Mesopotamia. The Sumerians, for instance, developed one of the earliest known systems of time measurement and calendrical systems based on astronomical observations.

It is important to approach ancient mythologies and their interpretations with caution, as they are often rich in symbolism, metaphor, and cultural context. While mythologies can provide insights into the beliefs and values of ancient societies, attributing specific preferences or aversions to deities like the Annunaki based on modern concepts, such as time schedules, may be speculative and not grounded in historical evidence.

In summary, the notion that the Annunaki harbored a dislike for strict time schedules is not supported by historical records or scholarly consensus. It is essential to separate the interpretations of ancient mythologies from modern concepts and understandings when exploring these topics.

4. Annunaki have always been portrayed as having stood against Lucifer in mythology.

The assertion that the Annunaki have consistently been depicted as standing against Lucifer in mythology is not accurate. It's important to note that the concept of Lucifer as a figure of evil or opposition to the divine has its origins in Christian theology, particularly in relation to the fallen angel mentioned in Christian scripture.

The Annunaki, on the other hand, originate from ancient Mesopotamian mythologies, specifically Sumerian and Babylonian cultures. In these mythologies, the Annunaki were a group of deities associated with various aspects of human life, rulership, and cosmic order. They were not typically portrayed as being in conflict with a figure resembling the Christian notion of Lucifer.

It's crucial to approach mythological comparisons and interpretations with care, as different cultures and belief systems have distinct mythological traditions and may assign different roles and characteristics to their deities.

While some individuals may draw connections or parallels between figures from different mythologies, it's important to recognize that these connections are often speculative and subject to individual interpretation. It is not accurate to claim a consistent portrayal of the Annunaki as standing against a figure similar to the Christian concept of Lucifer in ancient Mesopotamian mythologies.

Therefore, it is advisable to approach the subject with an understanding of the specific mythological contexts involved and the diverse interpretations that can arise when comparing different belief systems.

5. Annunaki don't like being referred to or compared to the other angels.

There is no historical or mythological evidence to suggest that the Annunaki had any specific preferences or dislikes regarding being referred to or compared to other angels. The concept of angels is primarily associated with Abrahamic religions, such as Judaism, Christianity, and Islam, and their respective theological beliefs and texts.

The Annunaki, on the other hand, originate from ancient Mesopotamian mythologies, specifically Sumerian and Babylonian cultures. In these mythologies, the Annunaki were a group of deities associated with various aspects of human life, cosmic order, and rulership. They were not typically depicted or referenced in the same context as the angels of Abrahamic traditions.

It is important to approach mythologies and religious beliefs within their specific cultural and historical contexts. Drawing direct comparisons or making assumptions about the preferences or dislikes of deities or divine beings from different mythological systems can be speculative and lacks a foundation in ancient sources.

While individuals may draw parallels or make connections between different mythologies and belief systems, it is essential to respect the diversity and distinctiveness of these traditions and avoid generalizations or assumptions about their beliefs, preferences, or interactions.

In summary, there is no evidence to suggest that the Annunaki had any specific aversion to being referred to or compared to other angels, as the concept of angels primarily belongs to Abrahamic religions, while the Annunaki originate from ancient Mesopotamian mythologies with their own distinct beliefs and mythological narratives.

6. Annunaki understanding of gravitation and physics would be beyond gifted.

The understanding of gravitation and physics attributed to the Annunaki is a speculative claim that lacks historical evidence or scientific support. The concept of the Annunaki originates from ancient Mesopotamian mythologies, and their portrayal does not provide specific indications of advanced knowledge in the field of physics or gravitation.

The understanding of gravitation and physics has evolved over centuries through scientific exploration and experimentation. It is a complex and intricate field of study that involves rigorous observation, mathematical modeling, and empirical evidence. Ancient civilizations, including those associated with the Annunaki, did not possess the scientific methodologies or technological advancements that have contributed to our modern understanding of these concepts.

Claims suggesting that ancient beings like the Annunaki possessed advanced knowledge of gravitation or physics often stem from speculative interpretations or fictional narratives that blend ancient mythologies with modern concepts. It is important to distinguish between historical mythologies and scientific knowledge when evaluating such claims.

In summary, there is no historical or scientific evidence to support the idea that the Annunaki had an advanced understanding of gravitation or physics. The understanding of these fields has developed through scientific inquiry and research over time, and attributing such knowledge to ancient civilizations is not supported by scholarly consensus or empirical evidence.

7. Annunaki are overly self conscious especially about their bodies.

There is no historical or mythological evidence to suggest that the Annunaki were overly self-conscious, particularly about their bodies. The concept of the Annunaki originates from ancient Mesopotamian mythologies, specifically Sumerian and Babylonian cultures. In these mythologies, the Annunaki were considered powerful deities associated with various aspects of human life, rulership, and cosmic order.

Ancient mythologies often focused on the actions and roles of deities within their cultural and religious contexts, and discussions of body image or self-consciousness were not typically prominent in these narratives.

It's important to approach ancient mythologies with an understanding of their cultural and historical contexts and not impose modern perspectives or concepts onto them. Ideas of body image, self-consciousness, or similar notions are shaped by the specific social and cultural dynamics of contemporary societies and may not align with ancient belief systems.

In summary, there is no basis in historical records or scholarly interpretations to support the claim that the Annunaki were overly self-conscious, particularly regarding their bodies. The emphasis of ancient mythologies was on the roles and attributes of these deities within the context of their respective civilizations.

8. Annunaki are capable of love, but it does not always serve them well.

The concept of love and its implications for the Annunaki, as portrayed in ancient Mesopotamian mythologies, is open to interpretation and may vary across different narratives and sources. The Annunaki, being deities associated with various aspects of human life and cosmic order, are often depicted in mythologies engaging in relationships, both romantic and familial, with other deities or humans.

While love and its consequences are themes found in many mythologies, it is important to note that the portrayal of love and its effects on the Annunaki can differ in different narratives and contexts. Ancient mythologies often used storytelling elements to convey moral, societal, or religious teachings rather than providing specific psychological or emotional profiles of deities.

It is worth noting that as mythological beings, the Annunaki are often depicted as having human-like characteristics, including emotions, desires, and relationships. However, attributing specific traits or behaviors to the Annunaki regarding the impact of love on their well-being would require a more detailed examination of specific mythological narratives and interpretations.

In summary, while love and its consequences are present in various mythologies, including those involving the Annunaki, the specific effects of love on the Annunaki can vary across different narratives and interpretations. The understanding of their relationships and emotional experiences is derived from ancient mythologies, which may not provide comprehensive or consistent portrayals of such concepts.

9. Annunaki are opinionated, but do not debate what they think or know is true.

The characterization of the Annunaki as opinionated but not engaging in debates over what they perceive as truth is not supported by historical records or scholarly consensus. The Annunaki, originating from ancient Mesopotamian mythologies, were a group of deities associated with various aspects of human life, rulership, and cosmic order.

While ancient mythologies often portrayed deities as having personal opinions or taking certain positions, the idea that the Annunaki did not engage in debates or discussions regarding their beliefs or knowledge is not explicitly mentioned in ancient texts.

It is important to approach ancient mythologies with an understanding of their cultural and historical contexts. The narratives and depictions of deities in these mythologies often served specific religious, cultural, or societal purposes, conveying moral or theological lessons rather than providing detailed insights into the nature of debates or discussions among the deities themselves.

Additionally, the concept of debates, as we understand them today, is shaped by the social and intellectual dynamics of contemporary societies. Applying modern notions of debate to ancient mythologies can lead to speculative interpretations and may not align with the original intentions or beliefs of the ancient cultures.

In summary, the claim that the Annunaki were opinionated but did not engage in debates over their beliefs or knowledge is not supported by historical records or scholarly consensus. Ancient mythologies focus on conveying moral or religious teachings, and the specifics of debates or discussions among deities are not typically detailed in these narratives.

10. Annunaki took the side of humanity in mythology.

In ancient Mesopotamian mythologies, the relationship between the Annunaki and humanity can vary depending on the specific narrative and context. While the Annunaki were revered as deities associated with various aspects of human life and rulership, their interactions with humanity were not consistently portrayed as unconditionally supportive.

In some myths, the Annunaki were credited with granting knowledge, culture, and advancements to humanity, playing a role in shaping human civilization. However, there are also narratives where the Annunaki's actions towards humans are depicted as capricious, demanding, or even punitive.

For example, in the Babylonian creation myth Enuma Elish, the Annunaki play a significant role in the establishment of cosmic order but are not explicitly portrayed as consistently taking the side of humanity. In other myths, such as the Epic of Gilgamesh, the actions of the Annunaki towards humanity are more nuanced and complex.

It is important to approach ancient mythologies with an understanding of their cultural and religious contexts. These narratives often served various purposes, including explaining natural phenomena, providing moral teachings, or reinforcing social hierarchies. The portrayal of the Annunaki's relationship with humanity can be influenced by these cultural and ideological considerations.

In summary, the relationship between the Annunaki and humanity in ancient Mesopotamian mythologies is multifaceted and varies across different narratives. While there are instances where the Annunaki are depicted as benefactors of humanity, it is not a consistent portrayal, and their interactions can be complex and nuanced in different mythological accounts.

11. Annunaki are very earthy, having a love of precious gems and metals.

In ancient Mesopotamian mythologies, the Annunaki are often associated with various aspects of human life, including the material realm. While they were revered as powerful deities, the specific portrayal of their affinity for precious gems and metals can vary across different narratives and sources.

Ancient Mesopotamian cultures, such as the Sumerians and Babylonians, valued precious gems and metals for their beauty, symbolism, and economic significance. These materials played a prominent role in their religious practices, adornment, and trade. It is not uncommon for deities in mythologies to be associated with elements of the natural world or highly prized materials.

While the Annunaki were not solely characterized by their love for precious gems and metals, their association with these materials can be found in certain mythological contexts. However, it is important to note that the emphasis on these materials in ancient mythologies is often symbolic and should not be interpreted as a direct reflection of the Annunaki's personal preferences or desires.

As with any interpretation of ancient mythologies, it is crucial to consider the cultural and historical context in which these narratives developed. Ancient societies often used symbolism and metaphor to convey deeper meanings, and the association of the Annunaki with precious gems and metals likely carries symbolic significance rather than a literal indication of their personal inclinations.

In summary, while the Annunaki can be associated with precious gems and metals in certain ancient Mesopotamian mythologies, it is important to understand this association within its cultural and symbolic context. The emphasis on these materials serves broader symbolic purposes and should not be taken as a direct representation of the Annunaki's personal preferences or characteristics.

12. Annunaki made one very big mistake in judging humanity.

In ancient Mesopotamian mythologies, the Annunaki are depicted as powerful deities involved in various aspects of human life and cosmic order. While there are different narratives surrounding the Annunaki's interactions with humanity, it is not explicitly stated that they made a singular significant mistake in judging humanity.

Mythological accounts often portray the relationship between the Annunaki and humanity as complex and multifaceted. There are instances where the Annunaki are depicted as benevolent beings who grant knowledge, culture, and advancements to humanity. However, there are also narratives where the Annunaki's actions towards humans are more ambivalent or even punitive, reflecting the challenges and tests faced by humanity.

It is worth noting that ancient mythologies contain symbolic and metaphorical elements that serve various purposes, such as providing moral teachings or explaining natural phenomena. As such, the notion of a singular "big mistake" made by the Annunaki in judging humanity may be a subjective interpretation or an element specific to certain modern retellings or interpretations of the mythologies.

To fully understand the nuances of the Annunaki's relationship with humanity, it is necessary to consider the wide range of mythological narratives and the cultural and religious context in which they originated. These narratives were shaped by the beliefs, values, and societal dynamics of ancient Mesopotamian civilizations.

In summary, while the Annunaki's interactions with humanity in ancient Mesopotamian mythologies can be complex, there is no explicit mention of a singular significant mistake made by the Annunaki in judging humanity. The portrayal of their relationship with humanity varies across different narratives and should be understood within the broader context of ancient mythologies.

13. Annunaki are naturally creative, and love creating useful new tools.

In ancient Mesopotamian mythologies, the Annunaki are often associated with various aspects of human life and civilization, including creativity and the development of useful tools. While the specific attributes and characteristics of the Annunaki can vary across different narratives, their role in fostering human creativity and technological advancements can be found in certain mythological contexts.

Ancient Mesopotamian civilizations, such as the Sumerians and Babylonians, made significant contributions to human innovation and technological progress. They were known for their advancements in agriculture, architecture, writing systems, and various crafts. These developments were often attributed to the influence or teachings of the deities, including the Annunaki.

The Annunaki, as powerful deities associated with different domains, were believed to inspire and guide human creativity. They were often credited with sharing knowledge, arts, and crafts with humanity, enabling the development of useful tools and technologies.

While ancient mythologies often contain symbolic and metaphorical elements, the association of the Annunaki with creativity and the creation of useful tools reflects the ancient Mesopotamian belief in the divine influence on human progress and civilization.

It is important to approach these mythological narratives with an understanding of their cultural and historical contexts. While the Annunaki's role in inspiring human creativity and the creation of tools is a recurring theme, it should not be interpreted as a direct reflection of their personal inclinations or abilities.

In summary, in ancient Mesopotamian mythologies, the Annunaki are associated with creativity and the development of useful tools. Their influence and guidance were believed to inspire human innovation and technological advancements. This portrayal reflects the cultural belief in the divine role in human progress and underscores the significance of the Annunaki in the mythology of ancient Mesopotamia.

14. Annunaki are natural inventors and teachers in many disciplines.

In ancient Mesopotamian mythologies, the Annunaki are often depicted as powerful deities associated with various aspects of human life and civilization. While the specific disciplines in which they are portrayed as inventors and teachers can vary across different narratives, the Annunaki are generally attributed with knowledge and expertise in diverse fields.

Ancient Mesopotamian civilizations made significant advancements in various disciplines, including astronomy, mathematics, agriculture, architecture, and writing systems. These achievements were often believed to be influenced or guided by the deities, including the Annunaki.

The Annunaki were revered as sources of wisdom and were associated with sharing knowledge and teaching humanity. They were believed to possess expertise in different disciplines and were regarded as inventors and innovators in various fields relevant to human life and civilization.

However, it is important to note that ancient mythologies often contain symbolic and metaphorical elements. The portrayal of the Annunaki as inventors and teachers in multiple disciplines should be understood within the broader context of mythological narratives and the cultural beliefs of ancient Mesopotamian societies.

While the Annunaki's role as inventors and teachers underscores their significance in the mythologies of ancient Mesopotamia, it is essential to approach these narratives with an understanding of their cultural and historical contexts. The specific disciplines and domains associated with the Annunaki's inventions and teachings can vary across different mythological accounts.

In summary, the Annunaki are often portrayed as natural inventors and teachers in various disciplines in ancient Mesopotamian mythologies. They are revered as sources of knowledge and wisdom, guiding humanity's advancements in different fields. However, the specifics of their expertise and the disciplines they are associated with can differ in different narratives and should be understood within the context of ancient mythologies.

15. Annunaki in war are likely to be consciencious objectors.

There is no specific mention or consensus in ancient Mesopotamian mythologies regarding the Annunaki being conscientious objectors in times of war. The Annunaki were revered as powerful deities associated with various aspects of human life and cosmic order, and their roles in mythological narratives can vary.

In ancient mythologies, deities often participate in conflicts and wars, taking sides or playing specific roles in battles. However, the specific attitudes or actions of the Annunaki as conscientious objectors in the context of warfare are not explicitly detailed in ancient Mesopotamian texts.

It is important to approach ancient mythologies with an understanding of their cultural and historical contexts. These mythologies often served various purposes, including explaining natural phenomena, providing moral teachings, or reinforcing societal norms. The emphasis on warfare in mythological narratives may serve symbolic or metaphorical purposes rather than providing insights into the Annunaki's stance as conscientious objectors.

Conscientious objection, as a concept related to personal beliefs and resistance to participating in armed conflicts, is rooted in modern ethical and legal frameworks. Applying this concept directly to the Annunaki, who existed in ancient mythologies, may not align with the beliefs and values of the ancient Mesopotamian cultures that developed these narratives.

In summary, there is no specific mention or consensus in ancient Mesopotamian mythologies regarding the Annunaki as conscientious objectors in times of war. The portrayal of the Annunaki in warfare in mythological narratives should be understood within the broader cultural and symbolic context of ancient Mesopotamian beliefs and values.

16. Annunaki are responsible for creating most weapons of modern war.

It is important to note that the concept of the Annunaki, originating from ancient Mesopotamian mythologies, predates modern warfare and the development of modern weapons by thousands of years. Therefore, attributing the creation of most weapons of modern war to the Annunaki is not supported by historical records, scholarly consensus, or scientific evidence.

Modern weapons have evolved through human technological advancements, scientific discoveries, and engineering innovations. The development of modern warfare and its associated weaponry is a result of human ingenuity, scientific research, and the progress of various civilizations throughout history.

Ancient mythologies, including those involving the Annunaki, often contain symbolic and metaphorical elements that serve cultural, religious, or moral purposes. While mythological narratives may include depictions of battles or conflicts involving deities, it is important to interpret them within their cultural and symbolic contexts rather than attempting to directly connect them to the development of modern weapons.

To understand the origins and advancements of modern warfare and weaponry, it is more appropriate to study human history, technological progress, military strategies, and scientific discoveries rather than looking to mythological narratives from ancient Mesopotamia.

In summary, the Annunaki, as depicted in ancient Mesopotamian mythologies, are not responsible for creating most weapons of modern war. The development of modern weaponry is the result of human ingenuity, scientific advancements, and historical progress over thousands of years. Ancient mythologies should be understood within their cultural and symbolic contexts, rather than attempting to directly attribute modern concepts to mythological beings.

17. Annunaki are unsure how to react to many human emotions.

In ancient Mesopotamian mythologies, the Annunaki are often portrayed as powerful deities with their own emotions and reactions. However, there is no specific mention or consensus regarding the Annunaki's uncertainty in reacting to human emotions.

Mythological narratives involving the Annunaki depict their interactions with humanity in various ways. They can display a range of emotions themselves, such as anger, compassion, or joy, and may respond differently to human emotions depending on the specific narrative.

While ancient mythologies offer insights into human experiences and emotions, the portrayal of the Annunaki's reactions to human emotions can vary across different narratives and should be understood within their cultural and mythological contexts.

It is important to approach ancient mythologies with an understanding that they often contain symbolic and metaphorical elements. The focus on emotions and the Annunaki's reactions in mythological accounts may serve broader purposes, such as conveying moral teachings or exploring the complexities of human-divine relationships, rather than providing direct insights into the Annunaki's uncertainties in reacting to specific human emotions.

In summary, there is no specific mention or consensus in ancient Mesopotamian mythologies regarding the Annunaki's uncertainty in reacting to human emotions. The portrayal of their interactions with human emotions can vary across different narratives and should be understood within the broader cultural and symbolic context of ancient mythologies.

18. Annunaki take things very personally and take rejection very hard.

In ancient Mesopotamian mythologies, the Annunaki are often depicted as powerful deities with their own personalities and reactions. While they can display a range of emotions, including anger, compassion, or joy, there is no specific mention or consensus regarding the Annunaki taking things personally or experiencing a particular difficulty with rejection.

Mythological narratives involving the Annunaki portray their interactions with humans in various ways. These interactions can involve granting favors, offering guidance, or even imposing punishments, depending on the specific narrative and context.

While the Annunaki's reactions to certain situations can be portrayed as personal, it is important to approach ancient mythologies with an understanding of their cultural and mythological contexts. The emphasis on personal reactions or the difficulty with rejection may serve symbolic or metaphorical purposes, conveying moral teachings or exploring the dynamics of human-divine relationships, rather than reflecting the Annunaki's personal experiences.

It is also worth noting that the portrayal of the Annunaki can vary across different narratives and sources. Different mythological accounts may present distinct characteristics or behaviors attributed to the Annunaki, reflecting the diversity of ancient Mesopotamian beliefs and interpretations.

In summary, while the Annunaki can display a range of emotions and reactions in ancient Mesopotamian mythologies, there is no specific mention or consensus regarding them taking things personally or struggling with rejection. The portrayal of their interactions with humans should be understood within the broader cultural and symbolic context of ancient mythologies, considering the diverse nature of mythological narratives and sources.

19. Annunaki are morally neutral, believing in sprituality and science.

In ancient Mesopotamian mythologies, the Annunaki are often depicted as powerful deities associated with various aspects of human life and cosmic order. While their specific moral inclinations can vary across different narratives, they are generally portrayed as beings with their own belief systems and understanding of spirituality and knowledge.

The ancient Mesopotamian civilizations had a complex religious and cosmological worldview, where spirituality and scientific observations coexisted. The Annunaki were believed to possess great wisdom and knowledge, which encompassed both spiritual and practical aspects.

In some mythological narratives, the Annunaki are portrayed as guides and teachers, sharing knowledge and wisdom with humanity. This can include scientific knowledge related to astronomy, agriculture, and other practical domains, as well as spiritual teachings and rituals.

However, it is important to note that ancient mythologies often contain symbolic and metaphorical elements. The concept of moral neutrality, as understood in modern ethical frameworks, may not directly apply to the Annunaki or ancient Mesopotamian mythologies. Their actions and behaviors are often depicted within the context of the larger cosmic order and the cultural values of the ancient Mesopotamian societies that developed these narratives.

In summary, the Annunaki in ancient Mesopotamian mythologies are depicted as powerful beings with their own belief systems encompassing spirituality and knowledge. They are associated with guiding and teaching humanity in various domains, including both practical and spiritual aspects. However, the notion of moral neutrality should be understood within the broader cultural and symbolic context of ancient Mesopotamian beliefs and values.

20. Annunaki are natural healers and often this power was misused.

In ancient Mesopotamian mythologies, the Annunaki are not typically associated with being natural healers. The concept of healing and medicine was attributed to other deities and specialized figures in the mythological narratives of ancient Mesopotamia.

In Mesopotamian belief systems, various deities and divine figures were associated with healing, such as the god Nergal, who was connected to the realm of health and disease. Additionally, there were specialized figures like the ashipu (exorcist) and the asu (physician), who were regarded as experts in healing practices and medicine.

While the Annunaki were revered as powerful deities with their own spheres of influence, the concept of them being natural healers or having a particular association with healing is not a prominent feature in ancient Mesopotamian mythologies.

However, mythological narratives often contain complex and multifaceted portrayals of deities, and different versions of myths may vary in their details. It is possible that in some specific narratives or interpretations, the Annunaki might have been depicted as having healing abilities or being associated with certain aspects of healing. Still, such instances would be less prevalent compared to other deities and figures specifically associated with healing and medicine.

In summary, while the Annunaki are not typically depicted as natural healers in ancient Mesopotamian mythologies, it is important to consider the diverse nature of mythological narratives and interpretations. Healing and medicine were generally attributed to other deities and specialized figures within the mythological framework of ancient Mesopotamia.

21. Annunaki believe in perfection, and actively seek it in everything.

In ancient Mesopotamian mythologies, the concept of the Annunaki actively seeking perfection in everything is not explicitly mentioned or widely attested. The Annunaki are typically portrayed as powerful deities associated with various aspects of human life and cosmic order, but their pursuit of perfection is not a central theme in their mythological depictions.

Ancient Mesopotamian cultures had diverse beliefs and mythologies that encompassed a range of themes, including human existence, societal order, and the relationships between deities and humans. While concepts of divine order, harmony, and balance were important in these belief systems, the specific notion of perfection as a primary goal for the Annunaki is not a prevailing motif.

It is worth noting that ancient mythologies often contain symbolic and metaphorical elements. The actions and behaviors of the Annunaki are typically depicted within the broader context of cosmic order and the cultural values of the ancient Mesopotamian societies that developed these narratives.

While seeking perfection or striving for excellence may be valued ideals in many human cultures, attributing these specific traits to the Annunaki in ancient Mesopotamian mythologies goes beyond the textual evidence available.

In summary, while the Annunaki are associated with aspects of human life and cosmic order in ancient Mesopotamian mythologies, the concept of actively seeking perfection in everything is not explicitly mentioned or widely attested. The portrayal of the Annunaki's actions and beliefs should be understood within the broader cultural and mythological context of ancient Mesopotamia.

22. Annunaki are easily corrupted by the quest for power.

In some ancient Mesopotamian mythologies, the Annunaki are portrayed as powerful deities with their own desires, motivations, and potential vulnerabilities. While not all narratives explicitly depict them as easily corrupted by the quest for power, there are instances where the pursuit of power can lead to negative consequences for the Annunaki.

Mythological narratives often explore the complexities of divine-human relationships and the consequences of certain actions or ambitions. Some stories may involve conflicts among the deities, including struggles for power or attempts to assert dominance over others.

In these narratives, the Annunaki, like other divine beings, can be influenced by their ambitions and desires. This can lead to moral dilemmas, rivalries, or instances where their actions have detrimental effects on themselves or others.

However, it is important to approach ancient mythologies with an understanding of their symbolic and metaphorical nature. The portrayal of the Annunaki's susceptibility to corruption should be understood within the broader cultural and mythological context of ancient Mesopotamia, rather than as a universal characteristic attributed to them in all narratives.

It is also worth noting that different mythological accounts may present varying portrayals of the Annunaki, reflecting the diversity of ancient Mesopotamian beliefs and interpretations.

In summary, while some ancient Mesopotamian mythologies depict instances where the Annunaki can be influenced by the quest for power, it is not a universal characteristic attributed to them in all narratives. The portrayal of their vulnerabilities and the consequences of their actions should be understood within the broader cultural and mythological context of ancient Mesopotamia, considering the diverse nature of mythological accounts and interpretations.

23. Annunaki are deeply aware of the world and its darkest problems.

In ancient Mesopotamian mythologies, the Annunaki are often depicted as powerful deities with a profound understanding of the world and its complexities. While the specific mention of them being aware of the world's darkest problems may not be prevalent in the available mythological texts, their knowledge and wisdom encompass various aspects of human existence.

The Annunaki are associated with cosmic order, divine governance, and the maintenance of balance in the world. They are often portrayed as beings with deep insights into the human condition, societal dynamics, and the intricate workings of the universe.

Their understanding of the world may include awareness of challenges, conflicts, and moral dilemmas faced by humans. While the emphasis on the world's darkest problems may vary across different narratives, the Annunaki's wisdom and knowledge encompass a broad range of human experiences and cosmic forces.

It is important to approach ancient mythologies with an understanding that they often contain symbolic and metaphorical elements. The focus on the Annunaki's awareness of the world's challenges may serve broader purposes, such as conveying moral teachings, highlighting the importance of maintaining order and balance, or exploring the dynamics of human-divine relationships.

In summary, while the specific mention of the Annunaki being aware of the world's darkest problems may not be prevalent in ancient Mesopotamian mythologies, they are generally depicted as beings with profound knowledge and understanding of the world and its intricacies. Their wisdom encompasses various aspects of human existence and cosmic order, serving broader purposes within the cultural and mythological context of ancient Mesopotamia.

24. Annunaki believe in the Law of One.

The belief in the Law of One is not a concept directly associated with the Annunaki in ancient Mesopotamian mythologies. The Law of One is a metaphysical and philosophical concept that emerged in modern spiritual and esoteric teachings, particularly through the works of Ra, a purported extraterrestrial entity channeled by L/L Research.

Ancient Mesopotamian mythologies encompass a rich array of beliefs, cosmologies, and religious systems, which may not align directly with the concepts introduced in modern spiritual teachings.

The Annunaki in ancient Mesopotamian mythologies are typically portrayed as powerful deities associated with various aspects of human life and cosmic order. Their roles and characteristics vary across different narratives, but the specific concept of the Law of One is not a prominent feature within their mythological framework.

It is important to recognize that ancient mythologies developed within specific cultural and historical contexts, and their beliefs and cosmologies should be understood within that framework. While the Law of One may resonate with certain contemporary spiritual beliefs, it does not have direct roots in ancient Mesopotamian mythologies or specifically associated with the Annunaki.

In summary, the belief in the Law of One is not a concept directly associated with the Annunaki in ancient Mesopotamian mythologies. The concept emerged in modern spiritual teachings and should be approached and understood within the context of those teachings rather than within the framework of ancient Mesopotamian beliefs and mythologies.

Author's Note:

Dear Reader,

As I bring this book to a close, I would like to express my deepest gratitude for joining me on this remarkable journey through the rise and fall of ancient civilizations, the exploration of the false matrix, and the celebration of the human spirit. It has been an honor to share these stories with you and to delve into the depths of history, mystery, and human resilience.

Throughout these pages, we have uncovered the hidden truths of the past, examined the intricate webs of deception, and marveled at the indomitable spirit of humanity. We have witnessed the grandeur of empires and civilizations, pondered the forces that shape our perception of reality, and celebrated the triumph of the human spirit in the face of adversity.

I hope that this book has ignited a spark within you—a curiosity to explore further, a desire to question the narratives that surround us, and a commitment to embracing the diversity and interconnectedness of our world. May it serve as a catalyst for deeper understanding, empathy, and positive change.

The stories we have explored are not merely tales of the past but powerful reflections of our present and potential guides for the future. By understanding the rise and fall of ancient civilizations, we can glean valuable lessons about the fragility of power, the consequences of unchecked ambition, and the importance of preserving the collective memory of humanity.

In parallel, the concept of the false matrix reminds us to remain vigilant in our pursuit of truth, to question the narratives presented to us, and to resist the allure of complacency. It challenges us to cultivate critical thinking, to seek diverse perspectives, and to navigate the complexities of our world with discernment.

Finally, the celebration of the human spirit resonates deeply within our souls. It reminds us of our capacity for resilience, hope, and transformative change. It invites us to tap into our inner strength, to stand up against injustice, and to create a future that reflects our shared values of compassion, equality, and progress.

As we bid farewell to the pages of this book, I encourage you to carry the stories, insights, and lessons with you on your own journey through life. Let them guide your actions, inform your choices, and inspire you to contribute positively to the world around you.

May the rise and fall of ancient civilizations, the exploration of the false matrix, and the celebration of the human spirit continue to fuel your curiosity, ignite your imagination, and remind you of the incredible tapestry of humanity we are all part of.

With heartfelt gratitude,

[David Jack Gregg]